NEW DIRECTIONS FOR EVALUATION
A Publication of the American Evaluation Association

Gary T. Henry, *Georgia State University*
COEDITOR-IN-CHIEF

Jennifer C. Greene, *University of Illinois*
COEDITOR-IN-CHIEF

Evaluation Models

Daniel L. Stufflebeam
Western Michigan University

AUTHOR

Number 89, Spring 2001

JOSSEY-BASS
San Francisco

EVALUATION MODELS
Daniel L. Stufflebeam (au.)
New Directions for Evaluation, no. 89
Jennifer C. Greene, Gary T. Henry, Coeditors-in-Chief

Microfilm copies of issues and articles are available in 16mm and 35mm, as well as microfiche in 105mm, through University Microfilms Inc., 300 North Zeeb Road, Ann Arbor, Michigan 48106-1346.

New Directions for Evaluation is indexed in Contents Pages in Education, Higher Education Abstracts, and Sociological Abstracts.

ISSN 1097-6736   ISBN 0-7879-5755-0

NEW DIRECTIONS FOR EVALUATION is part of The Jossey-Bass Education Series and is published quarterly by Jossey-Bass, 350 Sansome Street, San Francisco, California 94104-1342.

SUBSCRIPTIONS cost $66.00 for U.S./Canada/Mexico; $90 international. For institutions, agencies, and libraries, $130 U.S.; $170 Canada; $204 international. Prices are subject to change.

EDITORIAL CORRESPONDENCE should be addressed to the Editors-in-Chief, Jennifer C. Greene, Department of Educational Psychology, University of Illinois, 260E Education Building, 1310 South Sixth Street, Champaign, IL 61820, or Gary T. Henry, School of Policy Studies, Georgia State University, P.O. Box 4039, Atlanta, GA 30302-4039.

www.josseybass.com

Printed in the United States of America on acid-free recycled paper containing 100 percent recovered waste paper, of which at least 20 percent is postconsumer waste.

Editorial Policy and Procedures

New Directions for Evaluation, a quarterly sourcebook, is an official publication of the American Evaluation Association. The journal publishes empirical, methodological, and theoretical works on all aspects of evaluation. A reflective approach to evaluation is an essential strand to be woven through every volume. The editors encourage volumes that have one of three foci: (1) craft volumes that present approaches, methods, or techniques that can be applied in evaluation practice, such as the use of templates, case studies, or survey research; (2) professional issue volumes that present issues of import for the field of evaluation, such as utilization of evaluation or locus of evaluation capacity; (3) societal issue volumes that draw out the implications of intellectual, social, or cultural developments for the field of evaluation, such as the women's movement, communitarianism, or multiculturalism. A wide range of substantive domains is appropriate for *New Directions for Evaluation;* however, the domains must be of interest to a large audience within the field of evaluation. We encourage a diversity of perspectives and experiences within each volume, as well as creative bridges between evaluation and other sectors of our collective lives.

The editors do not consider or publish unsolicited single manuscripts. Each issue of the journal is devoted to a single topic, with contributions solicited, organized, reviewed, and edited by a guest editor. Issues may take any of several forms, such as a series of related chapters, a debate, or a long article followed by brief critical commentaries. In all cases, the proposals must follow a specific format, which can be obtained from the editor-in-chief. These proposals are sent to members of the editorial board and to relevant substantive experts for peer review. The process may result in acceptance, a recommendation to revise and resubmit, or rejection. However, the editors are committed to working constructively with potential guest editors to help them develop acceptable proposals.

Jennifer C. Greene, Coeditor-in-Chief
Department of Educational Psychology
University of Illinois
260E Education Building
1310 South Sixth Street
Champaign, IL 61820
e-mail:jcgreene@uiuc.edu

Gary T. Henry, Coeditor-in-Chief
School of Policy Studies
Georgia State University
P.O. Box 4039
Atlanta, GA 30302-4039
e-mail: gthenry@gsu.edu

CONTENTS

COEDITOR'S NOTES   1
Gary T. Henry

Evaluation Models   7
Daniel L. Stufflebeam

INDEX   99

COEDITOR'S NOTES

Professional evaluation is essentially about generating information that assists others in making judgments about a program, service, policy, organization, person, or whatever else is being evaluated. Over the past forty years, evaluation has developed out of a variety of activities to become a specialized field that relies on many different approaches for generating that information. It is important to continuously take stock and to ask which approaches should continue to be used and which should be laid aside. In this volume, Daniel L. Stufflebeam presents his analysis of twenty-two approaches that have guided the conduct of evaluation.

Stufflebeam analyzes twenty-two evaluation approaches that have been sufficiently well articulated and frequently used in making evaluative judgments about programs and services over the past forty or so years. He describes each approach, its orientation, purpose, typical questions being addressed, and methods. In many cases these approaches will be familiar to us by more than one label. Many times, he contrasts the approach being discussed with other approaches to illuminate what the approach is and is not.

However, his description of the approaches are but a prelude to the main event. Stufflebeam is true to his evaluator roots in applying his own systematic approach to the analysis of the twenty-two approaches. He takes the role of a connoisseur of evaluation and his perspective is *meta*-metaevaluation. He systematically assesses the approaches by rating them in each of four areas previously defined by the Joint Committee Program Evaluation Standards: utility, feasibility, propriety, and accuracy. These ratings are then combined to yield an overall score. Stufflebeam's extensive experience in conducting evaluations, his founding work with the Context, Input, Process, Product model, and his leadership in the development of evaluation standards gives him standing as a connoisseur of evaluation. The perspective he adopts could be considered doubly meta-evaluative in that he evaluates approaches to evaluation not specific evaluations.

In the end, Stufflebeam recommends that nine diverse approaches receive continued use. His analysis shows that these nine have very different strengths and few severe weaknesses. Some of Stufflebeam's conclusions reflect the working of the "survival of the fittest" in the evaluation field in that approaches such as clarification hearings came and went rather quickly. Other of his conclusions will be quite controversial, I suspect, such as his relatively low rating for program theory evaluation, which recently was the subject of an entire volume of *New Directions for Evaluation* (Petrosino, Rogers, Heubner, and Hasci, 2000). One virtue of the systematic process Stufflebeam has used is that it allows us to trace the specific ratings that landed a particular approach on the recommended list.

NEW DIRECTIONS FOR EVALUATION, no. 89, Spring 2001   © Jossey-Bass, A Publishing Unit of John Wiley & Sons, Inc.

In addition to providing you with a brief summary of what the article holds in store, I will explain how the volume came about, since it is unusual to have one article take up an entire volume. I also intend to offer some questions that Stufflebeam's analysis raised about evaluating evaluation approaches. In the conclusion, I suggest some possible venues for providing feedback and alternative perspectives on the variety of evaluation approaches currently in use.

How This Volume Came to Be

This volume represents only the second time since *New Directions for Evaluation* was launched, including the period from 1978 till 1995 when it was known as *New Directions for Program Evaluation,* that a volume has been devoted to one article by a single author. Although this represents a departure from our editorial policies, Coeditor-in-Chief Jennifer Greene and I have expressed our desire to be flexible in order to grasp opportunities that benefit our audience. We exercised that flexibility when we asked Daniel Stufflebeam to submit a manuscript for *New Directions for Evaluation.*

While scouting for potential contributions for *New Directions for Evaluation* at the American Educational Research Association meeting in the spring of 1999, I heard Dr. Stufflebeam present a preliminary, but very provocative version of the article that now appears in this volume. After several discussions about format, we decided that evaluators would benefit from a full treatment of the careful analysis that Stufflebeam presents here rather than cutting his presentation short to accommodate the traditional multiple-author format. We consider the use of this format a rare event and I will close these notes with some ideas about how we might present multiple perspectives on this work in the future in order to obtain the balance that we have sought during our editorship.

Pending Questions

From the moment that I grasped the scope of the analysis that Stufflebeam had undertaken and the boldness of his approach, I was ablaze with questions. In essence, he was asserting that evaluators should begin to winnow down their approaches to those that showed the most promise for assessing merit and worth, and be willing to put some approaches on the discard heap of history. In addition, while giving much room for others to develop alternative analyses to this end, Stufflebeam was ready to take a stand on how it could be done and to do it. Questions about Stufflebeam's analysis can be grouped into four categories:

1. How much does/should context matter in evaluating evaluation approaches?
2. Are there twenty-two approaches to evaluation?

3. What criteria should be used for evaluating the approaches?
4. What should we do with the findings?

Contextual Matters

Stufflebeam begins with a presumption that some evaluation approaches are better than others for evaluating any collection of services or activities that could be loosely described as a program. He defines evaluation as the assessment of merit and worth, then proceeds to analyze each approach based on its potential to yield a thorough assessment. There is much to recommend the adoption of a systematic approach to reduce the number of likely evaluation choices. For example, consider that resource constraints apply to evaluator training as well as to planning evaluations. The existence of these constraints begs for the list of possible choices to be winnowed down to the point that the most important entries on the list can each receive an appropriate share of the resources that are available. A question that presents itself is, Do we start with a general approach such as the one Stufflebeam has offered or do we begin by choosing among the branches on a decision tree defined by context and then climbing out as we consider alternative approaches?

It may be that assessing the merit and worth of Head Start for Congress and evaluating a Head Start service provider in Muscogee County, Georgia, would not begin with the same list of possible evaluation approaches. A national advisory panel recently recommended that a randomized experiment should be attempted to do the former and the approach was mandated in the request for proposals. A mixed methods approach may fare much better as an approach for the Muscogee County evaluation. But saying context will affect the assessment of the approaches can be akin to opening up the field to relativism that allows an anything goes attitude to prevail. Stufflebeam adroitly avoids the trap of relativism in his analysis, but context must surely serve to guide us through the recommended list to the adoption of one of the approaches.

Let Me Count the Ways (Evaluations Are Approached)

Stufflebeam presents a list of twenty-two approaches divided into four categories as his count of evaluation approaches. The list raises immediate questions. For example, what about the apparent absence of participatory evaluation? Cousins and Whitmore define two approaches within the participatory evaluation concept alone (1998). Are these adequately subsumed under constructivist approaches where Stufflebeam places empowerment evaluation for the purposes of his type of review? What about adding other newcomers, such as realistic evaluation (Pawson and Tilley, 1997), to the list? The list itself is likely to spawn numerous questions and alternative listings. In the end, if we are making progress as a profession, a highly desirable outcome could be a taxonomy of evaluation approaches around which there is a high degree of consensus.

The Criteria and the Standards

Stufflebeam employs a highly regarded and often used set of standards in his analysis, those of the Joint Committee on Standards for Educational Evaluation (1994). In compiling his assessment he weighted utility, feasibility, propriety, and accuracy equally. However, a poor rating on any of three accuracy standards or one propriety standard would have dropped an approach from the acceptable list. One question arises about the use of these standards as opposed to other standards that could be used as criteria, such as the Guiding Principles for Evaluators (Shadish, Newman, Scheirer, and Wye, 1995). However, I think few will object to the use of the Joint Committee standards as a valuable source for the analysis. But when the scores for the nine recommended approaches are analyzed further, accuracy was essentially tied with propriety for the lowest overall averages (mean = 77) and had the highest variation (s = 15). This may raise a question about the standard that an approach should achieve to receive commendation. Is "good" good enough? Does accuracy deserve special treatment as first among equals? Or does propriety?

Improve or Discard?

In his conclusions, Stufflebeam recommends nine approaches for continued use and development. The others seem, in absentia, to be "throwbacks." Accreditation is "on the bubble" and stays on the recommended list only if those who use it see fit to improve it. Here Stufflebeam reflects that classic and inevitable tension in deciding how to interpret evaluation findings. His approach reflects practical wisdom. Choose the alternatives from among those which are most likely to turnout good evaluations, work on improving those that could be made right, and discard those which are unlikely to be improved sufficiently to confidently be used to assess merit and worth. Should these results be viewed more with an eye to improving low scoring approaches or as an actionable assessment of merit and worth of the available approaches?

What Happens Now?

Stufflebeam has initiated a process that cries for a great deal of thought and deliberation. Because of the length of the article, other voices could not be simultaneously added to begin a dialogue. But, if you agree that Stufflebeam's analysis merits attention and consideration across the field, we invite you to take the next step. If enough interest is generated, a second volume of reactions and comments could be assembled. Perhaps, a panel at Evaluation 2001 could keep the discussion rolling. Proposals are often generated from conference sessions and Jennifer and I would be happy to receive one that adds more voices to the highly ambitious and very important start that Stufflebeam has begun.

References

Cousins, J. B., Whitmore, E. (1998). "Framing Participatory Evaluation" in Whitmore, E. (ed.) Understanding and Practicing Participatory Evaluation. New Directions for Evaluation, no. 80, San Francisco: Jossey-Bass.

Joint Committee on Standards for Educational Evaluation. (1994). "The Program Evaluation Standards, 2nd Ed." Newbury Park, CA: Sage Publications.

Pawson, R., Tilley, N. (1997). "Realistic Evaluation" Thousand Oaks, CA: Sage Publications.

Petrosino, A., Rogers, P., Heubner, T., and Hasci, T. (eds.) (2000). Program Theory Evaluation. New Directions for Evaluation, no. 88, San Francisco: Jossey-Bass.

Shadish, W. R., Newman, D. L., Scheirer, M. A., and Wye, C. (eds.). (1995). Guiding Principles for Evaluators. New Directions for Program Evaluation, no. 66, San Francisco: Jossey-Bass.

GARY T. HENRY is a professor in the Andrew Young School of Policy Studies, Department of Political Science, and Department of Education Policy Studies at Georgia State University.

Evaluation Models—Abstract

In entering a new millennium, it is a good time for evaluators to critically appraise their program evaluation approaches and decide which ones are most worthy of continued application and further development. It is equally important to decide which approaches are best abandoned. In this spirit, this monograph identifies and assesses twenty-two approaches often employed to evaluate programs. These approaches, in varying degrees, are unique and cover most program evaluation efforts. Two of the approaches, reflecting the political realities of evaluation, are often used illegitimately to falsely characterize a program's value and are labeled pseudo-evaluations. The remaining twenty approaches are typically used legitimately to judge programs and are divided into questions/methods-oriented approaches, improvement/accountability approaches, and social agenda/advocacy approaches. The best and most applicable of the program evaluation approaches appear to be Client-Centered/Responsive, Utilization-Focused, Decision/Accountability, Consumer-Oriented, Constructivist, Case Study, Outcome/Value-Added Assessment, and Accreditation, with the new Deliberative Democratic approach showing promise. The approaches judged indefensible or least useful were Politically Controlled, Public Relations, Accountability (especially payment by results), Clarification Hearing, and Program Theory-Based. The rest—including Objectives-Based, Experimental Studies, Management Information Systems, Criticism and Connoisseurship, Mixed Methods, Benefit-Cost analysis, Performance Testing, and Objective Testing Programs—were judged to have restricted though beneficial use in program evaluation. All legitimate approaches are enhanced when keyed to and assessed against professional standards for evaluations.[1]

[1] Appreciation is extended to colleagues who critiqued prior drafts of this monograph, especially Sharon Barbour, Gary Henry, Jerry Horn, Thomas Kellaghan, Gary Miron, Craig Russon, James Sanders, Sally Veeder, William Wiersma, and Lori Wingate. While their valuable assistance is acknowledged, the author is responsible for the monograph's contents and especially any flaws.

Evaluation Models[2]

Daniel L. Stufflebeam

Evaluators today have many more evaluation approaches available to them than in 1960. As they address the challenges of the 21st century, it is an opportune time to consider what 20th century evaluation developments are valuable for future use and which ones would best be left behind. I have, in this monograph, attempted to sort twenty-two alternative evaluation approaches into what fishermen sometimes call the "keepers" and the "throwbacks." More importantly, I have characterized each approach; assessed its strengths and weaknesses; and considered whether, when, and how it is best applied. The reviewed approaches emerged mainly in the U.S. between 1960 and 1999.

20th Century Expansion of Program Evaluation Approaches

Following a period of relative inactivity in the 1950s, a succession of international and national forces stimulated the expansion and development of evaluation theory and practice. The main influences were the efforts to vastly strengthen the U.S. defense system spawned by the Soviet Union's 1957 launching of Sputnik I; the new U.S. laws in the 1960s to equitably serve minorities and persons with disabilities; federal government evaluation requirements of the Great Society programs initiated in 1965; the U.S. movement begun in the 1970s to hold educational and social organizations accountable for both prudent use of resources and achievement of objectives; the stress on excellence in the 1980s as a means of increasing U.S. international competitiveness; and the trend in the 1990s for various organizations—both inside and outside the U.S.—to employ evaluation to ensure quality, competitiveness, and equity in delivering services. In pursuing reforms, American society has repeatedly pressed schools and colleges, health-care organizations, and various social welfare enterprises to show through evaluation whether or not services and improvement efforts were succeeding.

The development of program evaluation as a field of professional practice was also spurred by a number of seminal writings. These included, in chronological order, publications by Tyler (1942, 1950), Campbell and Stanley (1963), Cronbach (1963), Stufflebeam (1966, 1967), Tyler (1966), Scriven (1967), Stake (1967), Suchman (1967), Alkin (1969), Guba (1969),

[2] This monograph is a condensed and updated version of a manuscript prepared for the Western Michigan University Evaluation Center's Occasional Paper Series.

Provus (1969), Stufflebeam et al. (1971), Parlett and Hamilton (1972), Weiss (1972), House (1973), Eisner (1975), Glass (1975), Cook and Reichardt (1979), Cronbach and Associates (1980), House (1980), Patton (1980), Joint Committee on Standards for Educational Evaluation (1981), and Stake (1983). These and other authors/scholars began to project alternative approaches to program evaluation. Over the years, a rich literature on a wide variety of alternative program evaluation approaches developed. See, for example: Campbell, 1988; Chelimsky, 1987; Cook and Reichardt, 1979; Cousins and Earl, 1992; Cronbach, 1982; Fetterman, 1984, 1994; Greene, 1988; Guba and Lincoln, 1981, 1989; Joint Committee on Standards for Educational Evaluation, 1994; Levin, 1983; Madaus, Scriven, and Stufflebeam, 1983; Nave, Miech, and Mosteller, 2000; Nevo, 1993; Patton, 1982, 1990, 1994, 1997; Rossi and Freeman, 1993; Sanders, 1992; Schwandt, 1984, 1989; Scriven, 1991, 1993, 1994a, 1994b, 1994c; Shadish, Cook, and Leviton, 1991; Smith, M. F., 1986, 1989; Smith, N. L., 1987; Stake, 1975, 1986, 1988, 1995; Stufflebeam, 1997; Stufflebeam, Madaus, and Kellaghan, 2000; Stufflebeam and Shinkfield, 1985; Torres, 1991; Weiss, 1995; Whitmore, 1998; Wholey, Hatry, and Newcomer, 1995; Worthen and Sanders, 1987; Worthen, Sanders, and Fitzpatrick, 1997; and Yin, 1992.

Evaluation Models and Approaches

The monograph uses the term *evaluation approach* rather than *evaluation model* because the former is broad enough to cover illicit as well as laudatory practices. Also, beyond covering both creditable and noncreditable approaches, some authors of evaluation approaches say that the term *model* is too demanding to cover their published ideas about how to conduct program evaluations. But for these two considerations, the term *model* would have been used to encompass most of the evaluation proposals discussed in this monograph. This is so because most of the presented approaches are idealized or "model" views for conducting program evaluations according to their authors' beliefs and experiences.

Need to Study Alternative Approaches

The study of alternative evaluation approaches is important for professionalizing program evaluation and for its scientific advancement and operation. Professional, careful study of program evaluation approaches can help evaluators discredit approaches that violate sound principles of evaluation and legitimize and strengthen those that follow the principles. Scientifically, such a review can help evaluation researchers identify, examine, and address conceptual and technical issues pertaining to the development of the evaluation discipline. Operationally, a critical view of alternatives can help evaluators consider, assess, and selectively apply optional evaluation frameworks. The review also provides substance for evaluation training. The main values in studying alternative program evaluation approaches are to discover their strengths and weaknesses, decide which ones merit substantial use, determine when and how they are best applied, obtain direction for improving the approaches and devising better alternatives, and strengthen one's ability to conceptualize hybrid evaluation approaches.

The Nature of Program Evaluation

This monograph employs a broad view of program evaluation. It encompasses assessments of any coordinated set of activities directed at achieving goals. Examples are assessments of ongoing, cyclical programs, such as school curricula, food stamps, housing for the homeless, and annual influenza inoculations; time-bounded projects, such as development and dissemination of a fire prevention guide and development of a new instrument for evaluating the performance of factory workers; and national, regional, or state systems of services, such as those provided by regional educational service organizations and a state's department of natural resources. Program evaluations both overlap with and yet are distinguishable from other forms of evaluation, especially evaluations of students, personnel, materials, and institutions.

Previous Classifications of Alternative Evaluation Approaches

In analyzing the twenty-two evaluation approaches, prior assessments regarding program evaluation's state of the art were considered. Stake's (1974) analysis of nine program evaluation approaches provided a useful application of advance organizers (the types of variables used to determine information requirements) for ascertaining different types of program evaluations. Hastings' (1976) review of the growth of evaluation theory and practice helped to place the evaluation field in a historical perspective. Guba's (1990) book *The Paradigm Dialog* and his (1977) presentation and assessment of six major philosophies in evaluation were provocative. House's (1983) analysis of approaches illuminated important philosophical and theoretical distinctions. Scriven's (1991, 1994a) writings on the transdiscipline of evaluation helped to sort out different evaluation approaches; it was also invaluable in seeing the approaches in the broader context of evaluations focused on various objects other than programs. The book *Evaluation Models* (Madaus, Scriven, and Stufflebeam, 1983) provided a previous inventory and analysis of evaluation models.[3] All of the assessments helped sharpen the issues addressed.

---

[3]An extensive revised and updated edition of Evaluation Models (Stufflebeam, Madaus, & Kellaghan) published by Kluwer Academic Publishers in 2000.

Program Evaluation Defined

In characterizing and assessing evaluation approaches, the various kinds of activities conducted in the name of program evaluation were classified on the basis of their level of conformity to a particular definition of evaluation. In this monograph, evaluation means *a study designed and conducted to assist some audience to assess an object's merit and worth.* This definition should be widely acceptable since it agrees with common dictionary definitions of evaluation; it is also consistent with the definition that underlies published sets of professional standards for evaluations (Joint Committee on Standards for Educational Evaluation, 1981, 1988, 1994). However, it will become apparent that many studies done in the name of program evaluation either do not conform to this definition or directly oppose it.

Classification and Analysis of the Twenty-two Approaches

Using the above definition of evaluation, program evaluation approaches were classified into four categories. The first category includes approaches that promote invalid or incomplete findings (referred to as pseudoevaluations), while the other three include approaches that agree, more or less, with the definition (i.e., Questions and/or Methods-Oriented, Improvement/Accountability, and Social Agenda/Advocacy). Of the twenty-two program evaluation approaches that are described, two are classified as pseudoevaluations, thirteen as questions/methods-oriented approaches, three as improvement/ accountability-oriented approaches, and four as social agenda/advocacy approaches.

Each approach is characterized in terms of ten descriptors: (1) advance organizers, that is, the main cues that evaluators use to set up a study; (2) main purpose(s) served; (3) sources of questions addressed; (4) questions that are characteristic of each study type; (5) methods typically employed; (6) persons who pioneered in conceptualizing each study type; (7) other persons who have extended development and use of each study type; (8) key considerations in determining when to use each approach; (9) strengths of the approach; and (10) weaknesses of the approach. Comments on each of the twenty-two program evaluation approaches are presented.

The Questions/Methods-Oriented approaches, Improvement/Account-ability-Oriented approaches, and the Social Agenda/Advocacy Approaches are also contrasted in tables keyed to six of the descriptors: advance orga-nizers, primary evaluation purposes, characteristic evaluation questions, main evaluation methods, prevalent strengths, and prevalent weaknesses/ limitations. These tables were reviewed in reaching conclusions about which approaches should be avoided and which are most meritorious.

Nine approaches that appeared most worthy were then selected for a consumers report type analysis. These approaches were evaluated against the requirements of the Joint Committee (1994) *Program Evaluation*

Standards to obtain judgments—of Poor, Fair, Good, Very Good, or Excellent—of each approach's utility, feasibility, propriety, accuracy, and overall merit. The judgments of each of the nine approaches were reached using a specially prepared checklist.[4] For each of the thirty Joint Committee standards, the checklist contained ten checkpoints representing the standard's key requirements. The author rated each evaluation approach on each of the thirty Joint Committee program evaluation standards by judging whether the approach—as defined in the literature and otherwise known to the author—satisfactorily addresses each of the 10 checkpoints. Regardless of each approach's total score and overall rating, I would have attached a notation of unacceptable to any approach receiving a rating of poor on any one of the vital standards of P1 Service Orientation, A5 Valid Information, A10 Justified Conclusions, and A11 Impartial Reporting. I rated the approaches based on my knowledge of the Joint Committee Program Evaluation Standards, my many years of studying the various evaluation models and approaches, and my experience in seeing and assessing how some of these models and approaches worked in practice. I chaired the Joint Committee on Standards for Educational Evaluation during its first thirteen years and led the development of the first editions of both the program and personnel evaluation standards.

Caveats

I acknowledge, without apology, that the assessments of the approaches and the entries in the summary charts in this monograph are based on my best judgments. I have taken no poll, and no definitive research exists, to represent a consensus on the characteristics, strengths and weaknesses, and comparative merits of the different approaches. I also acknowledge my conflict of interest, since I was one of the developers of one of the rated approaches: Decision/Accountability. My analyses reflect thirty-five years of experience in applying and studying different evaluation approaches. Hopefully, these analyses will be useful to evaluators and evaluation students at least in the form of working hypotheses to be tested.

I have mainly looked at the approaches as relatively discrete ways to conduct evaluations. In reality, there are many occasions when it is functional to mix and match different approaches. A careful analysis of such combinatorial applications no doubt would produce several hybrid approaches that might merit examination. That analysis is beyond the scope of this monograph.

---

[4]This checklist and an abbreviated version of it are available at the following Web location <www.wmich.edu/evalctr/checklists>.

Pseudoevaluations

Because this monograph is focused on describing and assessing the state of the art in evaluation, it is necessary to discuss bad and questionable practices, as well as best efforts. Evaluators and their clients are sometimes tempted to shade, selectively release, or even falsify findings. While such efforts might look like sound evaluations, they are aptly termed *pseudoevaluations* if they fail to produce and report valid assessments of merit and worth to all right-to-know audiences.

Pseudoevaluations often are motivated by political objectives. For example, persons holding or seeking authority may present unwarranted claims about their achievements and/or the faults of their opponents or hide potentially damaging information. These objectionable approaches are presented because they deceive through evaluation and can be used by those in power to mislead constituents or to gain and maintain an unfair advantage over others, especially persons with little power. If evaluators acquiesce to and support pseudoevaluations, they help promote and support injustice, mislead decision making, lower confidence in evaluation services, and discredit the evaluation profession.

I identified two pseudoevaluation approaches, labeled Public Relations-Inspired Studies and Politically Controlled Studies. They are primarily distinguished on the matters of truth seeking and dissemination of findings. Public relations studies do not seek truth but instead acquire and broadcast information that provides a favorable, though often false impression of a program. Politically controlled studies seek the truth but inappropriately control the release of findings to right-to-know audiences.

Approach 1: Public Relations-Inspired Studies. The public relations approach begins with an intention to use data to convince constituents that a program is sound and effective. Other labels for the approach are "ideological marketing" (see Ferguson, June 1999), advertising, and infomercial. The public relations approach may meet the standard for addressing all right-to-know audiences but fails as a legitimate evaluation approach, because typically it presents a program's strengths, or an exaggerated view of them, but not its weaknesses.

Tom Clancy and General Chuck Horner (1999, p. 501) gave poignant examples of public relations studies that were supposedly but not really conducted to gain valuable lessons from the 1991 Gulf War called Desert Storm.

> In the United States, the Joint Chiefs of Staff and each of the service departments published 'Lessons Learned' documents that were in fact advertisements for individual programs, requirements, or services . . . the so-called 'studies' tended to be self-supporting rather than critical of the agency that sponsored the work. And too many of the books, monographs, studies, and official documents misstated the facts, with the aim of salvaging a weapon system, military doctrine, or reputation whose worth could not otherwise be supported. They were public relations documents, not clear-eyed honest

appraisals, and they were aimed at influencing the soon-to-come budget reductions and debates over each service's roles and missions.

The advance organizer of the public relations study is the propagandist's information needs. The study's purpose is to help a program's leaders or public relations personnel project a convincing, positive public image for a program. The guiding questions are derived from the public relations specialists' and administrators' conceptions of which questions constituents would find most interesting. In general, the public relations study seeks information that would most help an organization confirm its claims of excellence and secure public support. From the start, this type of study seeks not a valid assessment of merit and worth, but information to help the program "put its best foot forward." Such studies avoid gathering or releasing negative findings.

Typical methods used in public relations studies are biased surveys; inappropriate use of norms tables; biased selection of testimonials and anecdotes; "massaging" of obtained information; selective release of only the positive findings; reporting central tendency, but not variation; cover-up of embarrassing incidents; and the use of "expert" advocate consultants. In contrast to the "critical friends" employed in Australian evaluations, public relations studies use "friendly critics." A pervasive characteristic of the public relations evaluator's use of dubious methods is a biased attempt to nurture a good picture for a program. The fatal flaw of built-in bias to report only good things offsets any virtues of this approach. If an organization substitutes biased reporting of only positive findings for balanced evaluations of strengths and weaknesses, it soon will demoralize evaluators who are trying to conduct and report valid evaluations and may discredit its overall practice of evaluation.

By disseminating only positive information on a program's performance while withholding information on shortcomings and problems, evaluators and clients may mislead taxpayers, constituents, and other stakeholders concerning the program's true value and what issues need to be addressed to make it better. The possibility of such positive bias in advocacy evaluations underlies the longstanding policy of Consumers Union not to include advertising by the owners of the products and services being evaluated in its *Consumer Reports* magazine. To maintain credibility with consumers, Consumers Union has, for the most part, maintained an independent perspective and a commitment to identify and report both strengths and weaknesses in the items evaluated and not to supplement this information with biased ads. (An exception is that the magazine advertises its own supplementary publications and services, without presenting clear, independent evaluations of them.)

Evaluators need to be cautious in how they relate to the public relations activities of their sponsors, clients, and supervisors. Certainly, public relations documents will reference information from sound evaluations. Evaluators should do what they can to persuade their audiences to make honest use of the evaluation findings. Evaluators should not be party to misuses, especially in cases where erroneous reports are issued that predictably will mislead readers to believe that a seriously flawed program is effective. As one safeguard, evaluators can promote and help their clients arrange to have independent metaevaluators examine the organization's production and use of evaluation findings against professional standards for evaluations.

Approach 2: Politically Controlled Studies. The politically controlled study is an approach that can be either defensible or indefensible. A politically controlled study is illicit if the evaluator and/or client (a) withhold the full set of evaluation findings from audiences who have express, legitimate, and legal rights to see the findings; (b) abrogate their prior agreement to fully disclose the evaluation findings; or (c) bias the evaluation message by releasing only part of the findings. It is not legitimate for a client first to agree to make the findings of a commissioned evaluation publicly available and then, having previewed the results, to release none or only part of the findings. If and when a client or evaluator violates the formal written agreement on disseminating findings or applicable law, then the other party has a right to take appropriate actions and/or seek an administrative or legal remedy.

Clients sometimes can legitimately commission covert studies and keep the findings private, while meeting relevant laws and adhering to an appropriate advance agreement with the evaluator. This can be the case in the United States for private organizations not governed by public disclosure laws. Furthermore, an evaluator, under legal contractual agreements, can plan, conduct, and report an evaluation for private purposes, while not disclosing the findings to any outside party. The key to keeping client-controlled studies in legitimate territory is to reach appropriate, legally defensible, advance, written agreements and to adhere to the contractual provisions concerning release of the study's findings. Such studies also have to conform to applicable laws on release of information.

The advance organizers for a politically controlled study include implicit or explicit threats faced by the client for a program evaluation and/or objectives for winning political contests. The client's purpose in commissioning such a study is to secure assistance in acquiring, maintaining, or increasing influence, power, and/or money. The questions addressed are those of interest to the client and special groups that share the client's interests and aims. Two main questions are of interest to the client: What is the truth, as best can be determined, surrounding a particular dispute or political situation? What information would be advantageous in a potential conflict situation? Typical methods of conducting the politically controlled study include covert investigations, simulation studies, private polls, private information files, and selective release of findings. Generally, the client wants information that is as technically sound as possible. However, he or she may also want to withhold findings that do not support his or her position. The strength of the approach is that it stresses the need for accurate information. However, because the client might release information selectively to create or sustain an erroneous picture of a program's merit and worth, might distort or misrepresent the findings, might violate a prior agreement to fully release findings, or might violate a "public's right to know" law, this type of study can degenerate into a pseudoevaluation.

Inappropriate politically controlled studies undoubtedly contributed to the federal and state sunshine laws in the United States. Under current U.S. and state freedom of information provisions, most information obtained through the use of public funds must be made available to interested and potentially affected citizens. Thus, there exist legal deterrents to and remedies for illicit, politically controlled evaluations that use public funds.

While it would be unrealistic to recommend that administrators and other evaluation users not obtain and selectively employ information for political gain, evaluators should not lend their names and endorsements to evaluations presented by their clients that misrepresent the full set of relevant findings, that present falsified reports aimed at winning political contests, or that violate applicable laws and/or prior formal agreements on release of findings. Despite these warnings, it can be legitimate for evaluators to give private evaluative feedback to clients, provided they conform with pertinent laws, statutes, policies, and sound contractual agreements on release of findings are reached and honored.

Questions- and Methods-Oriented Evaluation Approaches (Quasi-Evaluation Studies)

Questions-oriented program evaluation approaches address specified questions (often employing a wide range of methods), and methods-oriented approaches typically use a particular method. Whether the methodology and questions addressed in these approaches are appropriate for assessing a program's merit and worth is a secondary consideration. I have grouped the questions- and methods-oriented approaches together, because they both tend to narrow an evaluation's scope. The first two approaches discussed (objectives-based studies and accountability studies) are mainly questions-oriented approaches, while the other eleven approaches in this section are methods-oriented approaches.

The questions-oriented approaches usually begin with a set of narrowly defined questions. These might be derived from a program's behavioral/operational objectives, a funding agency's pointed accountability requirements, or an expert's preferred set of evaluative criteria. The methods-oriented approach may employ as its starting point a design for a controlled experiment, a particular standardized test, a cost-analysis procedure, a theory or model of a program, case study procedures, or a management information system. Another kind of methods-oriented approach is the study that starts with an overriding commitment to employ a mixture of qualitative and quantitative methods. The methods-oriented approaches emphasize technical quality. Both the methods-oriented and questions-oriented approaches stress that it is usually better to answer a few pointed questions well than to attempt a broad assessment of a program's merit and worth.

Both the questions- and methods-oriented approaches can be called quasi-evaluation studies, because sometimes they happen to provide evidence that fully assesses a program's merit and worth, while in most cases their focus is too narrow or is only tangential to questions of merit and worth. While the approaches are typically labeled as evaluations, they may or may not meet all the requirements of a sound evaluation. Quasi-evaluation studies have legitimate uses apart from their relationship to program evaluation, since they can investigate important though narrow questions. The main caution is that these types of studies not be uncritically equated to evaluation.

Approach 3: Objectives-Based Studies. The objectives-based study is the classic example of a questions-oriented evaluation approach. Madaus and Stufflebeam (1988) provided a comprehensive look at this approach by publishing an edited volume of the classical writings of Ralph W. Tyler. In this approach, some statement of objectives provides the advance organizer. The objectives may be mandated by the client, formulated by the evaluator, or specified by the service providers. Typically, the objectives-oriented evaluation is an internal study done by a curriculum developer or other program leader. The usual purpose of an objectives-based study is to determine whether the program's objectives have been achieved. Usual audiences are program developers, sponsors, and managers who want to know the extent to which each stated objective was achieved.

The methods used in objectives-based studies essentially involve specifying operational objectives and collecting and analyzing pertinent information to determine how well each objective was achieved. Tyler stressed that a wide range of objective and performance assessment procedures usually should be employed. This sets his approach apart from those methods-oriented studies that focus on a particular method, such as an experimental design or a particular standardized test. Criterion-referenced tests and students' work samples are especially relevant to this evaluation approach.

Ralph Tyler is generally acknowledged to be the pioneer in the objectives-based type of study, although Percy Bridgman and E. L. Thorndike should also be credited (Travers, 1977). Several people have furthered Tyler's seminal contribution by developing variations of his evaluation model. They include Bloom et al. (1956), Hammond (1972), Metfessel and Michael (1967), Popham (1969), Provus (1971), and Steinmetz (1983).

The objectives-based approach is especially applicable in assessing tightly focused projects that have clear, supportable objectives. Even then, such studies can be strengthened by judging project objectives against the intended beneficiaries' assessed needs, searching for side effects, and studying the process as well as the outcomes.

The objectives-based study has been the most prevalent approach in program evaluation. It has common-sense appeal; program administrators have had a great amount of experience with it; and it makes use of technologies of behavioral objectives, both norm-referenced and criterion-referenced testing, and performance assessments. Common criticisms are that such studies lead to terminal information that is neither timely nor pertinent to improving a program's process; that the information often is far too narrow to constitute a sufficient basis for judging the object's merit and worth; that the studies do not uncover positive and negative side effects; and that they may credit unworthy objectives.

Approach 4: Accountability, Particularly Payment by Results Studies. The accountability/payment by results approach is a questions-oriented approach and typically narrows the evaluative inquiry to questions about outcomes. In contrast to the objectives-based studies—which also focus on outcomes—accountability studies stress the importance of obtaining an external, impartial perspective as contrasted to the internal perspective often preferred in Tylerian, objectives-based studies. Accountability studies became prominent in the early 1970s. They emerged because of widespread disenchantment with the persistent stream of evaluation reports indicating that almost none of the massive state and federal investments in educational and social programs were making any positive, statistically discernable differences. One proposed solution advocated initiating externally administered accountability systems to ensure both that service providers would fulfill their responsibilities to improve services and that evaluators would find the programs' effects and determine which persons and groups were succeeding and which were not. Key components of many accountability systems are their employment of pass/fail standards, payment for good results, and sanctions for unacceptable performance.

The advance organizers for the accountability study are the persons and groups responsible for producing results, the service providers' work responsibilities, the expected outcomes, pass/fail cut scores, and defined consequences of passing or failing. The study's purposes are to provide constituents with an accurate accounting of results; ensure, through something akin to intimidation, that the results are primarily positive; determine responsibility for good and bad outcomes; and take appropriate actions. Accountability questions come from the program's constituents and controllers, such as taxpayers; parent groups; school boards; legislators; and local, state, and national funding organizations. Their main question concerns whether each funded organization charged with responsibility for delivering and improving services is carrying out its assignments and achieving all it should, given the resources invested to support the work.

Typical of other questions-oriented evaluation approaches, accountability studies have employed a wide variety of methods. These include procedures for setting pass/fail standards; payment by results; performance contracting; Management by Objectives (MBO); program input, process, output databases; Program Planning and Budgeting Systems (PPBS); institutional report cards/profiles; audits of procedural compliance and goal achievement; self-studies; peer reviews focused on established criteria; merit pay for organizations, programs, and/or individuals; and mandated testing programs. Also included are awards, recognition, sanctions, and takeover/intervention authority by oversight bodies.

Lessinger (1970) is generally acknowledged as a pioneer in the area of accountability. Among those who have extended Lessinger's work are Stenner and Webster (1971), in their development of a handbook for conducting auditing activities, and Kearney, in providing leadership to the Michigan Department of Education in developing the first statewide educational accountability system. Kirst (1990) analyzed the history and diversity of attempts at accountability in education within the following six broad types of accountability: performance reporting, monitoring and compliance with standards or regulations, incentive systems, reliance on the market, changing locus of authority or control of schools, and changing professional roles. A recent major attempt at accountability, involving financial rewards and sanctions, was the Kentucky Instructional Results Information System (Koretz and Barron, 1998). This program's failure was clearly associated with fast pace implementation in advance of validation, reporting and later retraction of flawed results, test results that were not comparable to those in other states, payment by results that fostered teaching to tests and cheating in schools, and heavy expense associated with performance assessments that could not be sustained over time.

Accountability approaches are applicable to organizations and professionals funded and charged to carry out public mandates, deliver public services, and implement specially funded programs. It behooves these program leaders to maintain a dynamic baseline of information needed to demonstrate fulfillment of responsibilities and achievement of positive results. They especially should focus accountability mechanisms on program elements that can be changed with the prospect of improving outcomes. They should also focus accountability to enhance staff cooperation toward achievement of collective goals rather than to intimidate or stimulate counterproductive competition. Moreover, accountability studies that compare programs should fairly consider the programs' contexts, especially beneficiaries' characteristics and needs, local support, available resources, and external forces.

The main advantages of accountability studies are that they are popular among constituent groups and politicians and are aimed at improving public services. They can also provide program personnel with clear expectations against which to plan, execute, and report on their services and contributions. They can be designed to give service providers freedom to innovate on procedures coupled with clear expectations and requirements for producing and reporting on accomplishments. Further, setting up healthy, fair competition between comparable programs can result in better services and products for consumers. Accountability studies typically engage program personnel to record and show their achievements and outsiders to provide an independent assessment of accomplishments.

A main disadvantage is that accountability studies often result in invidious comparisons and thereby produce unhealthy competition and much political unrest and acrimony among service providers and between them and their constituents. Also, accountability studies often focus on a too limited set of outcome indicators and can undesirably narrow the range of services. Another disadvantage is that politicians tend to force the implementation of accountability efforts before the needed instruments, scoring rubrics, assessor training, etc., can be planned, developed, field-tested, and validated. Furthermore, prospects for rewards and threats of punishment have often led service providers to cheat in order to assure positive evaluation reports. In schools, cheating to obtain rewards and avoid sanctions has frequently generated bad teaching, bad press, turnover in leadership, and abandonment of the accountability system.

I turn next to three approaches grounded in educational testing. For those outside the field of education, my inclusion of these approaches may seem strange. I have included them for two main reasons. First, program evaluation in its early history drew much of its theory and procedures from experiences in evaluating schools and school programs. Second, educational tests have continued to be a principal means of assessing the merit and worth of schools. This was patently clear in the recent presidential election campaigns wherein both principal candidates called for assessing and rewarding schools based on student scores from national or state tests.

Approach 5: Objective Testing Programs. Since the 1930s, American elementary and secondary schools have been inundated with standardized, multiple choice, norm-referenced testing programs. Probably every school district in the country has some such program. The tests are administered annually by local school districts and/or state education departments to inform students, parents, educators, and the public at large about the achievements of children and youth. The purposes of testing are to assess the achievements of individual students and groups of students compared with norms and/or standards. Typically, tests are administered to all students at selected grade levels. Because the test results focus on student outcomes and are conveniently available, many educators have tried to use the results to evaluate the quality of special projects, specific school programs, schools, and even individual educators by inferring that high scores reflect successful efforts and low scores reflect poor efforts. Such inferences can be wrong if the tests were not targeted on particular project or program objectives or the needs of particular target groups of students, if students' background characteristics were not taken into account, if certain students were inappropriately excluded from the testing, if resources and administrative support were not considered, etc.

Advance organizers for standardized educational tests include areas of the school curriculum, curricular objectives, and specified norm groups. The testing programs' main purposes are to compare the test performance scores of individual students and groups of students to those of selected norm groups and/or to diagnose shortfalls related to particular objectives. Standardized test results are also often used to compare the performance of programs and schools and to examine achievement trends across years. Metrics used to make the comparisons typically are standardized individual and mean scores and/or percentage of objectives passed for the total test and subtests. The sources of test questions are usually test publishers and test development/selection committees.

The typical question addressed by testing is whether the test performance of individual students is at or above the average performance of local, state, and national norm or comparison groups. Other questions may concern the percentages of students who surpassed one or more cut-score standards, where the group of students ranks compared to similar groups, and whether achievement is better than in prior years. The main process is to select, administer, score, analyze, interpret, and report the tests.

Lindquist (1951), a major pioneer in this area, was instrumental in developing the Iowa testing programs, the American College Testing Program, the National Merit Scholarship Testing Program, and the General Educational Development Testing Program, as well as the Measurement Research Center at the University of Iowa. Many individuals have contributed substantially to the development of educational testing in America, including Ebel (1965), Flanagan (1939), Lord and Novick (1968), and Thorndike (1971). Innovations in testing in the 1980s and 1990s include the development of item response theory (Hambleton and Swaminathan, 1985) and value-added measurement (Sanders and Horn, 1994; Webster, 1995).

If a school's personnel carefully select tests and use them appropriately to assess and improve student learning and report to the public, the involved expense and effort are highly justified. Student outcome measures for judging specific projects and programs must be validated in terms of the particular objectives and the characteristics and needs of the students served by the program. However, tests should not be relied on exclusively for evaluating specially targeted projects and programs. Results should be interpreted in light of other information on student characteristics, students' assessed needs, program implementation, student participation, and other outcome measures.

The main advantages of standardized testing programs are that they are efficient in producing valid and reliable information on student performance in many areas of school curricula and that they are a familiar strategy at every level of the school program in virtually all school districts in the United States. The main limitations are that they provide data only about student outcomes; they reinforce students' multiple-choice test-taking behavior rather than their writing and speaking behaviors; they tend to address only lower-order learning objectives; and, in many cases, they are perhaps a better indicator of the socioeconomic levels of the students in a given program, school, or school district than of the quality of teaching and learning. Stake (1971) and others have argued effectively that standardized tests often are poor approximations of what teachers actually teach. Moreover, as has been patently clear in evaluations of programs for both disadvantaged and gifted students, norm-referenced tests often do not measure achievements well for low and high scoring students. Unfortunately, program evaluators often have made uncritical use of standardized test results to judge a program's outcomes, just because the results were conveniently available and had face validity for the public. Often, the contents of such tests do not match the program's objectives.

A recent study by the center I direct illustrates the nature and limitations of an Objective Testing type of evaluation. The National Education Association contracted The Evaluation Center to evaluate the student achievement results at charter schools operated by a particular school management company. The study's director, Dr. Gary Miron, analyzed all the available standardized test data he could obtain for ten schools, which are spread across six states. He examined the scores for each school against pertinent state and national norms and results for the local school district housing the charter school. He looked at achievement trends and also compared his findings with those of other test score-based evaluations of the company-managed schools. In many cases, his findings were at odds with those of other evaluators, especially the company's evaluator. In general, Dr. Miron's study provided an in-depth look at the available test score evidence and how the charter school students performed in comparison to norms and selected comparison groups. He also assessed whether student test score gains in the charter schools met or exceeded expectations based on state and national norms tables. While Dr. Miron's study provided important evidence on student achievement in the charter schools, a number of factors limited his study from being a full evaluation. Much of the needed test score data was missing and Dr. Miron could not determine whether certain students were excluded from the tests or whether the schools' attrition rates were abnormally high. Also, he could not evaluate the merit and worth of the charter schools program, because he mainly had student test score data, which is only one facet of a school program's quality; had too little information on curriculum, teacher quality, materials, parent involvement, etc.; and looked only at a nonrandom sample of the schools being managed by the company.

Approach 6: Outcome Evaluation as Value-Added Assessment. Systematic, recurrent outcome/value-added assessment, coupled with hierarchical gain score analysis is a special case of the use of standardized testing to evaluate the effects of programs and policies. The emphasis is often on annual testing at all or a succession of grade levels to assess trends and partial out effects of the different components of an education system, including groups of schools, individual schools, and individual teachers. The intent is to determine what value each entity is adding to the achievements of students served by particular components of the education system and then report the results for policy, accountability, and improvement purposes. The main interest is in aggregates, not performance of individual students.

A state education department may annually collect achievement data from all students (at a succession of grade levels), as is the case in the Tennessee Value-Added Assessment System. The evaluator may analyze the data to look at contrasting gain score trends for different schools. Results may be further broken out to make comparisons between curricular areas, teachers, elementary versus middle schools, size and resource classifications of schools, districts, and areas of a state. What differentiates the approach from the typical standardized achievement testing program is the emphasis on sophisticated gain score and hierarchical analysis of data to delineate effects of system components and identify which ones should be improved and which ones should be commended and reinforced. Otherwise, the two approaches have much in common.

Advance organizers in outcome evaluation employing value-added analysis are systemwide indicators of intended outcomes and a scheme for obtaining, classifying, and analyzing gain scores. The purposes of outcome/value-added assessment systems are to provide direction for policymaking, accountability to constituents, and feedback for improving programs and services. The approach requires standardization of assessment data throughout a system. The questions to be addressed by outcome/value-added evaluations originate from governing bodies, policymakers, the system's professionals, and constituents. In reality, the questions are often limited by the data available from the tests regularly used by the state or school district.

Developers of the outcome/value-added assessment approach include Sanders and Horn (1994); Webster (1995); Webster, Mendro, and Almaguer (1994); and Tymms (1995). Questions that address this form of evaluation follow: To what extent are particular programs adding value to students' achievements? What are the cross-year trends in outcomes? In what sectors of the system is the program working best and poorest? What are key, pervasive shortfalls in particular program objectives that require further study and attention? To what extent are program successes and failures associated with the system's groupings of grade levels (e.g., primary, middle or junior high, and high school)?

Outcome monitoring involving value-added assessment is probably most appropriate in well-financed state education departments and large school districts having strong support from policy groups, administrators, and service providers. The approach requires system-wide buy-in; politically effective leaders to continually explain and sell the program; annual testing at a succession of grade levels; a smoothly operating, dynamic, computerized baseline of relevant input and output information; highly skilled technicians to make it run efficiently and accurately; a powerful computer system; complicated, large-scale statistical analysis; and high-level commitment to use the results for policy development, accountability, program evaluation, and improvement at all levels of the system.

The central advantage of outcome monitoring involving value-added assessment is in the systematization and institutionalization of a database of outcomes that can be used over time and in a standardized way to study and find means to improve outcomes. This approach makes efficient use of standardized tests; is amenable to analysis of trends at state, district, school, and classroom levels; uses students as their own controls; and emphasizes that students at all ability levels should be helped to grow in knowledge and skills. The approach is conducive to using a standard of continuous progress across years for every student, as opposed to employing static cut scores. The latter, while prevalent in accountability programs, basically fail to take into account meaningful gains by low or high achieving students, since such gains usually are far removed from the static, cut score standards. Sanders and Horn (1994) have shown that use of static cut scores may produce a "shed pattern," in which students who began below the cut score make the greatest gains while those who started above the cut score standard make little progress. Like the downward slope, from left to right, of a tool shed, the gains are greatest for previously low scoring students and progressively lower for the higher achievers. This suggests that teachers may be concentrating mainly on getting students to the cut score standard but not beyond it, thus holding back the high achievers.

A major disadvantage of the outcome/value-added approach is that it is politically volatile, since it is used to identify responsibility for successes and failures down to the levels of schools and teachers. It is also heavily reliant on quantitative information such as that coming from standardized, multiple-choice achievement tests. Consequently, the complex and powerful analyses are based on a limited scope of outcome variables. Nevertheless, Sanders (1989) has argued that a strong body of evidence supports the use of well-constructed, standardized, multiple-choice achievement tests. Beyond the issue of outcome measures, the approach does not provide in-depth documentation of program inputs and processes and makes little if any use of qualitative methods. Despite advancements in objective measurement and the employment of hierarchical mixed models to determine effects of a system's organizational components and individual staff members, critics of the approach argue that causal factors are so complex that no measurement and analysis system can fairly fix responsibility for the academic progress of individual and collections of students to the level of teachers. Also, personal experience in interviewing educators in all of the schools in a Tennessee school district—subject to the statewide Tennessee value-added student assessment program—showed that none of the teachers, administrators, and counselors interviewed understood or trusted the fairness of this approach.

Approach 7: Performance Testing. In the 1990s, major efforts were made to offset the limitations of typical multiple-choice tests by employing performance or authentic measures. These devices require students to demonstrate their achievements by producing authentic responses to evaluation tasks, such as written or spoken answers, musical or psychomotor presentations, portfolios of work products, or group solutions to defined problems. Arguments for performance tests are that they have high face validity and model and reinforce students' needed life skills. After all, students are not being taught so that they will do well in choosing best answers from a list, but so that they will master underlying understandings and skills and effectively apply them in real life situations.

The advance organizers in performance assessments are life-skill objectives and content-related performance tasks, plus ways that their achievement can be demonstrated in practice. The main purpose of performance tasks is to compare the performance of individual students and groups of students to model performance on the tasks. Grades assigned to each respondent's performance, using set rubrics, enables assessment of the quality of achievements represented and comparisons across groups.

The sources of questions addressed by performance tests are analyses of selected life-skill tasks and content specifications in curricular materials. The typical assessment questions concern whether individual students can effectively write, speak, figure, analyze, lead, work cooperatively, and solve given problems up to the level of acceptable standards. The main testing process is to define areas of skills to be assessed; select the type of assessment device; construct the assessment tasks; determine scoring rubrics; define standards for assessing performance; train and calibrate scorers; validate the measures; and administer, score, interpret, and report the results.

In speaking of licensing tests, Flexner (1910) called for tests that ascertain students' practical ability to successfully confront and solve problems in concrete cases. Some of the pioneers in applying performance assessment to state education systems were the state education departments in Vermont and Kentucky (Kentucky Department of Education, 1993; Koretz & Barron, 1998, 1996; Koretz and Barron, 1998). Other sources of information about the general approach and issues in performance testing include Baker, O'Neil, and Linn (1993); Herman, Gearhart, and Baker (1993); Linn, Baker, and Dunbar (1991); Mehrens (1972); Messick (1994); Stillman, Haley, Regan, Philbin, Smith, O'Donnell, and Pohl (1991); Swanson, Norman, and Linn (1995); Torrance (1993); and Wiggins (1989).

It is often difficult to establish the necessary conditions to employ the performance testing approach. It requires a huge outlay of time and resources for development and application. Typically, state education departments and school districts should probably use this approach very selectively and only when they can make the investment needed to produce valid results that are worth the large, required investment. On the other hand, students' writing ability is best assessed and nurtured through obtaining, assessing, and providing critical feedback on their writing.

One advantage of performance tests is minimization of guessing. Requiring students to construct responses to assessment tasks also reinforces writing, computation, scientific experimentation, and other life skills.

Major disadvantages of the approach are the heavy time requirements for administration; the high costs of scoring; the difficulty in achieving reliable scores; the narrow scope of skills that can feasibly be assessed; and lack of norms for comparisons, especially at the national level. In general, performance tests are inefficient, costly, and often of dubious reliability. Moreover, compared with multiple-choice tests, performance tests, in the same amount of testing time, cover a much narrower range of questions. The nation's largest attempt to install and operate a state accountability system grounded almost totally in performance assessments was the Kentucky Instructional Results Information System (KIRIS). The program failed and at this writing is being largely replaced with a program of multiple choice, standardized tests.

Approach 8: Experimental Studies. In using controlled experiments, program evaluators randomly assign beneficiaries (such as students or groups of students or patients) or organizations (such as schools or hospitals) to experimental and control groups and then contrast the outcomes after the experimental group received a particular intervention and the control group received no special treatment or some different treatment. This type of study was quite prominent in program evaluations during the late 1960s and early 1970s, when there were federal requirements to assess the effectiveness of federally funded innovations in schools and social service organizations. However, experimental program evaluations subsequently fell into disfavor and disuse. Apparent reasons for this decline are that educators, social workers, and other social service providers rarely can meet the required experimental conditions and assumptions.

This approach is labeled a quasi-evaluation strategy because it starts with questions and a methodology that address only a narrow set of program issues. Experimental methods do not investigate a target population's needs or the particulars of a program's process. Experimental and quasi experiments are insufficient to address the full range of questions required to assess a program's merit and worth.

In the 1960s, Campbell and Stanley (1963) and others hailed the true experiment as the best and preferred means of evaluating interventions. Many evaluators interpreted this message to mean that they should use only true experiments to evaluate social and education innovations. They often ignored the additional advice that Campbell and Stanley had advanced concerning quasi-experimental designs that could be used acceptably, though not ideally, when a true experiment was not feasible.

This piece of evaluation history is reminiscent of Kaplan's (1964) famous warning against the so-called "law of the instrument," whereby a given method is equated to a field of inquiry. In such a case, the field of inquiry is restricted to the questions that are answerable by the given method and the conditions required to apply the method. Fisher (1951) specifically warned against equating his experimental methods with science.

In general, experimental design is a method that can contribute importantly to program evaluation, as Nave, Miech, and Mosteller (2000) have demonstrated. However, as they also found, education and social programs evaluators rarely have conducted sound and useful experiments.

The advance organizers in experimental studies are problem statements, competing treatments, hypotheses, investigatory questions, and randomized treatment and comparison groups. The usual purpose of the controlled experiment is to determine causal relationships between specified independent and dependent variables, such as between a given instructional method and student standardized-test performance. It is particularly noteworthy that the sources of questions investigated in the experimental study are researchers, program developers, and policy figures, and not usually a program's constituents and staff.

The frequent question in the experimental study is, What are the effects of a given intervention on specified outcome variables? Typical methods used are experimental and quasi-experimental designs. Pioneers in using experimentation to evaluate programs are Campbell and Stanley (1963), Cronbach and Snow (1969), Lindquist (1953), and Suchman (1967). Others who have developed the methodology of experimentation substantially for program evaluation are Boruch (1994), Glass and Maguire (1968), and Wiley and Bock (1967).

Evaluators should consider conducting a controlled experiment only when its required conditions and assumptions can be met. Often this requires substantial political influence, substantial funding, and widespread agreement—among the involved funders, service providers, and beneficiaries—to submit to the requirements of the experiment. Such requirements typically include, among others, a stable program that will not have to be studied and modified during the evaluation; the ability to establish and sustain comparable program and control groups; the ability to keep the program and control conditions separate and uncontaminated; and the ability to obtain the needed criterion measures from all or at least a representative group of the members of the program and comparison groups. Evaluability assessment was developed as a particular methodology for determining the feasibility of moving ahead with an experiment (Smith, 1989; Wholey, 1995).

Controlled experiments have a number of advantages. They focus on results and not just intentions or judgments. They provide strong methods for establishing relatively unequivocal causal relationships between treatment and outcome variables, something that can be especially significant when program effects are small but important. Moreover, because of the prevalent use and success of experiments in such fields as medicine and agriculture, the approach has widespread credibility.

These advantages, however, are offset by serious objections to experimenting on school students and other human subjects. It is often considered unethical or even illegal to deprive control group members of the benefits of special funds for improving services. Likewise, many parents do not want schools or other organizations to experiment on their children by applying unproven interventions. Typically, schools find it impractical and unreasonable to randomly assign students to treatments and to hold treatments constant throughout the study period. Furthermore, experimental studies provide a much narrower range of information than organizations often need to assess and strengthen their programs. On this point, experimental studies tend to provide terminal information that is not useful for guiding the development and improvement of programs and may in fact thwart ongoing modifications of programs.

An example of a failed field experiment is seen in a personnel experience that occurred in a Great Society-era federal program. In the early 1970s, I served on a metaevaluation team charged to monitor and evaluate the federally mandated and funded experimental design-based evaluation of the Emergency School Assistance Act program (ESAA). This program provided federal funds to help certain school districts serve a recent dramatic increase of students in the districts. This increase stemmed mainly from a huge Vietnam War-related buildup of military personnel stationed near certain school districts.

In that period of accountability, Congress required federally supported programs to be evaluated. Experimental design advocates had persuaded Congress to mandate, within the ESAA legislation, that ESAA be evaluated by means of a true experiment. With a federal award of about $5 million— a very large sum then—the evaluation contractor designed and proceeded to implement a true experiment in each of several ESAA school districts. The focal question was To what extent does an allocation of ESAA funds to certain qualifying schools in each district increase student achievement and other outcomes beyond those seen in equivalent qualifying district schools not receiving ESAA funds? Members of matched pairs of qualifying schools in each district were randomly assigned to ESAA support or no ESAA support.

Although highly qualified experimental design experts planned and conducted the study and had $5 million at their disposal, they did not satisfactorily answer the study's main question. After the first year, there were no significant differences in the outcome variables of interest. It was found that the experimental and control schools were receiving approximately the same level of per-pupil expenditures. Further investigation revealed that as soon as a school district's leaders had learned which of the qualifying schools in the district had been randomly assigned to the ESAA allocation of federal funds, they diverted other local funds to the district's control schools. The district leaders' motivation for doing this seemed clearly aimed at avoiding community controversy over providing unequal support to all the deserving schools. Since there were no significant differences between experimental and control conditions (amount of money per student), there was no prospect for finding a significant difference in student outcomes attributable to the ESAA investment. Ironically, to rescue the evaluation the evaluators hastily converted it to a set of case studies.

While some field-based experiments have produced useful information, the above case shows that—even with a Congressional mandate, much money, and experimental design experts—it can be extremely difficult to meet the requirements of true experiments in field settings. Politics and other unexpected and uncontrollable interferences often impede the success of field experiments in dynamic areas, such as educational innovation. Even if the ESAA experiment had succeeded, it would have provided far less information about what the schools did with the money—the important treatments beyond federal funds—than did the case studies. If the ESAA evaluators had attempted to evaluate the much more complex but relevant treatments—e.g., instructional methods and materials, in-service training for teachers, counseling of students, parent involvement, administrative support—rather than just federal money, they probably would have had little chance of learning much of importance through an experimental approach.

Educators should not presuppose that an experiment is the best or even an acceptable approach in all program evaluation situations. In my experience, experimentally oriented evaluations can be workable and useful under the right circumstances. However, in education and human services, such circumstances are rare.

Approach 9: Management Information Systems. Management Information Systems are like politically controlled approaches, except that they supply managers with information needed to conduct and report on their programs, as opposed to supplying them with information needed to win a political advantage. The management information approach is also like the decision/accountability-oriented approach, which will be discussed later, except that the decision/accountability-oriented approach provides information needed to both develop and defend a program's merit and worth, which goes beyond providing information that managers need to implement and report on their management responsibilities. The payment by results/accountability approach, described previously, also should not be confused with the management information system approach. While both approaches maintain a base of information that can be used for accountability, the latter approach includes no scheme for payment by results and sanctions.

The advance organizers in most management information systems include program objectives, specified activities, projected program milestones or events, and a program budget. A management information system's purpose is to continuously supply managers with the information they need to plan, direct, control, and report on their programs or spheres of responsibility.

The sources of questions addressed are the management personnel and their superiors. The main questions they typically want answered are, Are program activities being implemented according to schedule, according to budget, and with the expected results? To provide ready access to information for addressing such questions, systems regularly store and make accessible up-to-date information on program goals, planned operations, actual operations, staff, program organization, expenditures, threats, problems, publicity, and achievements.

Methods employed in management information systems include system analysis, Program Evaluation and Review Technique (PERT), Critical Path Method, Program Planning and Budgeting System (PPBS), Management by Objectives (MBO), computer-based information systems, periodic staff progress reports, and regular budgetary reporting.

Cook (1966) introduced the use of PERT to education, and Kaufman (1969) wrote about the use of management information systems in education. Business schools and programs in computer information systems regularly provide courses in management information systems. These focus mainly on how to set up and employ computerized information banks for use in organizational decision making.

W. Edwards Deming (1986) argued that managers should pay close attention to process rather than being preoccupied with outcomes. He advanced a systematic approach for monitoring and continuously improving an enterprise's process, arguing that close attention to the process will result in increasingly better outcomes. It is commonly said that, in paying attention to this and related advice from Deming, Japanese carmakers and, later, American carmakers greatly increased the quality of automobiles (Aguaro, 1990). Bayless and Massaro (1992) applied Deming's approach to program evaluations in education.

In observing an attempt by a renowned national expert in Deming's methods to apply the approach in some Florida schools, I concluded that the approach, as applied there, failed. This seemed to be because the industry-based method is not well suited to assessing the complexities of educational processes. Unlike the manufacture of automobiles, educators have no definitive, standardized models for linking exact educational processes to specified outcomes and must address the needs of students possessing a wide range of individual differences.

Nevertheless, given modern database technology, program managers often can and should employ management information systems in multiyear projects and programs. Program databases can provide information, not only for keeping programs on track, but also for assisting in the broader study and improvement of program processes and outcomes.

A major advantage of the use of management information systems is in giving managers information they can use to plan, monitor, control, and report on complex operations. A difficulty with the application of this industry-oriented type of system to education and other social services, however, is that the products of many programs are not amenable to a narrow, precise definition as is the case with a corporation's profit and loss statement or its production of standardized products. Moreover, processes in educational and social programs often are complex and evolving rather than straightforward and uniform like those of manufacturing and business. The information gathered in management information systems typically lacks the scope of context, input, process, and outcome information required to assess a program's merit and worth.

Approach 10: Benefit-Cost Analysis Approach. Benefit-cost analysis as applied to program evaluation is a set of largely quantitative procedures used to understand the full costs of a program and to determine and judge what these investments returned in objectives achieved and broader social benefits. The aim is to determine costs associated with program inputs, determine the monetary value of the program outcomes, compute benefit-cost ratios, compare the computed ratios to those of similar programs, and ultimately judge a program's productivity in economic terms.

The benefit-cost analysis approach to program evaluation may be broken down into three levels of procedure: (1) cost analysis of program inputs, (2) cost-effectiveness analysis, and (3) benefit-cost analysis. These may be looked at as a hierarchy. The first type, cost analysis of program inputs, may be done by itself. Such analyses entail an ongoing accumulation of a program's financial history, which is useful in controlling program delivery and expenditures. The program's financial history can be used to compare its actual and projected costs and how costs relate to the costs of similar programs. Cost analyses can also be extremely valuable to outsiders who might be interested in replicating a program.

Cost-effectiveness analysis necessarily includes cost analysis of program inputs to determine the cost associated with progress toward achieving each objective. For example, two or more programs' costs and successes in achieving the same objectives might be compared. A program could be judged superior on cost-effectiveness grounds if it had the same costs but superior outcomes as similar programs. Or a program could be judged superior on cost-effectiveness grounds if it achieved the same objectives as more expensive programs. Cost-effectiveness analyses do not require conversion of outcomes to monetary terms but must be keyed to clear, measurable program objectives.

Benefit-cost analyses typically build on a cost analysis of program inputs and a cost-effectiveness analysis. But the benefit-cost analysis goes further. It seeks to identify a broader range of outcomes than just those associated with program objectives. It examines the relationship between the investment in a program and the extent of positive and negative impacts on the program's environment. In doing so, it ascertains and places a monetary value on program inputs and each identified outcome. It identifies a program's benefit-cost ratios and compares these to similar ratios for competing programs.

Ultimately, benefit-cost studies seek conclusions about the comparative benefits and costs of the examined programs.

Advance organizers for the overall benefit-cost approach are associated with cost breakdowns for both program inputs and outputs. Program input costs may be delineated by line items (e.g., personnel, travel, materials, equipment, communications, facilities, contracted services, overhead), by program components, and by year. In cost-effectiveness analysis, a program's costs are examined in relation to each program objective, and these must be clearly defined and assessed. The more ambitious benefit-cost analyses look at costs associated with main effects and side effects, tangible and intangible outcomes, positive and negative outcomes, and short-term and long-term outcomes—both inside and outside a program. Frequently, they also may break down costs by individuals and groups of beneficiaries. One may also estimate the costs of foregone opportunities and, sometimes, political costs. Even then, the real value of benefits associated with human creativity or self-actualization are nearly impossible to estimate. Consequently, the benefit-cost equation rests on dubious assumptions and uncertain realities.

The purposes of these three levels of benefit-cost analysis are to gain clear knowledge of what resources were invested, how they were invested, and with what effect. In popular vernacular, cost-effectiveness and benefit-cost analyses seek to determine the program's bang for the buck. There is great interest in answering this type of question. Policy boards, program planners, and taxpayers are especially interested to know whether program investments are paying off in positive results that exceed or are at least as good as those produced by similar programs. Authoritative information on the benefit-cost approach may be obtained by studying the writings of Kee (1995), Levin (1983), and Tsang (1997).

Benefit-cost analysis is potentially important in most program evaluations. Evaluators and their clients are advised to discuss this matter thoroughly with their clients, to reach appropriate advance agreements on what should and can be done to obtain the needed cost information, and to do as much cost-effectiveness and benefit-cost analysis as can be done well and within reasonable costs.

Benefit-cost analysis is an important but problematic consideration in program evaluations. Most evaluations are amenable to analyzing the costs of program inputs and maintaining a financial history of expenditures. The main impediment is that program authorities often do not want anyone other than the appropriate accountants and auditors looking into their financial books. If cost analysis, even at only the input levels, is to be done, this must be clearly provided for in the initial contractual agreements covering the evaluation work. Performing cost-effectiveness analysis can be feasible if cost analysis of inputs is agreed to; if there are clear, measurable program objectives; and if comparable cost information can be obtained from competing programs. Unfortunately, it is usually hard to meet all these conditions. Even more unfortunate is the fact that it is usually impractical to conduct a thorough benefit-cost analysis. Not only must it meet all the conditions of the analysis of program inputs and cost-effectiveness analysis, it must also place monetary values on identified outcomes, both anticipated and unexpected.

Approach 11: Clarification Hearing. The clarification hearing is one label for the judicial approach to program evaluation. The approach essentially puts a program on trial. Role-playing evaluators competitively implement both a damning prosecution of the program—arguing that it failed—and a defense of the program—arguing that it succeeded. A judge hears arguments within the framework of a jury trial and controls the proceedings according to advance agreements on rules of evidence and trial procedures. The actual proceedings are preceded by the collection of and sharing of evidence by both sides. The prosecuting and defending evaluators may call witnesses and place documents and other exhibits into evidence. A jury hears the proceedings and ultimately makes and issues a ruling on the program's success or failure. Ideally, the jury is composed of persons representative of the program's stakeholders. By videotaping the proceedings, the administering evaluator can, after the trial, compile a condensed videotape as well as printed reports to disseminate what was learned through the process.

The advance organizers for a clarification hearing are criteria of program effectiveness that both the prosecuting and defending sides agree to apply. The main purpose of the judicial approach is to ensure that the evaluation's audience will receive balanced evidence on a program's strengths and weaknesses. The key questions essentially are, Should the program be judged a success or failure? Is it as good or better than alternative programs that address the same objectives?

Robert Wolf (1975) pioneered the judicial approach to program evaluation. Others who applied, tested, and further developed the approach include Levine (1974), Owens (1973), and Popham and Carlson (1983). Steven Kemis (Stake, 1999, p. 333) recently conducted a "metaevaluation court" to assess Robert Stake's (Stake, 1999, pp. 323–343) evaluation of Reader Focused Writing for the Veterans Benefits Administration. Essentially, Kemis sought to " . . . raise and address questions about matters which might throw doubt on the dependability of the findings of the CIRCE study."

Based on the past uses and evaluations of this approach, it can be judged as only marginally relevant to program evaluation. Because of its adversarial nature, the approach encourages evaluators to present biased arguments in order to win their cases. Thus, truth seeking is subordinated to winning. The most effective debaters are likely to convince the jury of their position even when it is poorly founded. The approach is also politically problematic, since it generates considerable acrimony. Despite the attractiveness of using the law, with its attendant rules of evidence, as a metaphor for program evaluation, its promise has not been fulfilled. There are few occasions in which it makes practical sense for evaluators to apply this approach.

Approach 12: Case Study Evaluations. Program evaluation that is based on a case study is a focused, in-depth description, analysis, and synthesis of a particular program or other object. The investigators do not control the program in any way. Rather, they look at it as it is occurring or as it occurred in the past. The study looks at the program in its geographic, cultural, organizational, and historical contexts, closely examining its internal operations and how it uses inputs and processes to produce outcomes. It examines a wide range of intended and unexpected outcomes. It looks at the program's multiple levels and also holistically at the overall program. It characterizes both central dominant themes and variations and aberrations. It defines and describes the program's intended and actual beneficiaries. It examines beneficiaries' needs and the extent to which the program effectively addressed the needs. It employs multiple methods to obtain and integrate multiple sources of information. While it breaks apart and analyzes a program along various dimensions, it also provides an overall characterization of the program.

The main thrust of the case study approach is to delineate and illuminate a program, not necessarily to guide its development or to assess and judge its merit and worth. Hence, this monograph characterizes the case study approach as a questions/methods-oriented approach rather than an improvement/accountability approach.

Advance organizers in case studies include the definition of the program, characterization of its geographic and organizational environment, the historical period in which it is to be examined, the program's beneficiaries and their assessed needs, the program's underlying logic of operation and productivity, and the key roles involved in the program. A case study program evaluation's main purpose is to provide stakeholders and their audiences with an authoritative, in-depth, well-documented explication of the program.

The case study should be keyed to the questions of most interest to the evaluation's main audiences. The evaluator must therefore identify and interact with the program's stakeholders. Along the way, stakeholders will be engaged to help plan the study and interpret findings. Ideally, the audiences include the program's oversight body, administrators, staff, financial sponsors, beneficiaries, and potential adopters of the program.

Typical questions posed by some or all of the above audiences are, What is the program in concept and practice? How has it evolved over time? How does it actually operate to produce outcomes? What has it produced? What are the shortfalls and negative side effects? What are the positive side effects? In what ways and to what degrees do various stakeholders value the program? To what extent did the program effectively meet beneficiaries' needs? What were the most important reasons for the program's successes and failures? What are the program's most important unresolved issues?

How much has it cost? What are the costs per beneficiary, per year, etc.? What parts of the program have been successfully transported to other sites? How does this program compare with what might be called critical competitors? These questions only illustrate the range of questions that a case study might address, since each study will be tempered by the interests of the client and other audiences for the study and the evaluator's interests.

To conduct effective case studies, evaluators need to employ a wide range of qualitative and quantitative methods. These may include analysis of archives; collection of artifacts, such as work samples; content analysis of program documents; both independent and participant observations; interviews; logical analysis of operations; focus groups; tests; questionnaires; rating scales; hearings; forums; and maintenance of a program database. Reports may incorporate in-depth descriptions and accounts of key historical trends; focus on critical incidents, photographs, maps, testimony, relevant news clippings, logic models, and cross-break tables; and summarize main conclusions. The case study report may include a description of key dimensions of the case, as determined with the audience, as well as an overall holistic presentation and assessment. Case study reports may involve audio and visual media as well as printed documents.

Case study methods have existed for many years and have been applied in such areas as anthropology, clinical psychology, law, the medical profession, and social work. Pioneers in applying the method to program evaluation include Campbell (1975), Lincoln and Guba (1985), Platt (1992), Smith and Pohland (1974), Stake, Easely, and Anastasiou (1978), Stake (1995), and Yin (1992).

The case study approach is highly appropriate in program evaluation. It requires no controls of treatments and subjects and looks at programs as they naturally occur and evolve. It addresses accuracy issues by employing and triangulating multiple perspectives, methods, and information sources. It employs all relevant methods and information sources. It looks at programs within relevant contexts and describes contextual influences on the program. It looks at programs holistically and in depth. It examines the program's internal workings and how it produces outcomes. It includes systematic procedures for analyzing qualitative information. It can be tailored to focus on the audience's most important questions. It can be done retrospectively or in real time. It can be reported to meet given deadlines and subsequently updated based on further developments. The power of the case study approach is enhanced when multiple case studies are conducted within a programmatic area.

The main limitation of the case study is that some evaluators may mistake its openness and lack of controls as an excuse for approaching it haphazardly and bypassing steps to ensure that findings and interpretations possess rigor as well as relevance. Furthermore, because of a preoccupation with descriptive information, the case study evaluator may not collect sufficient judgmental information to permit a broad-based assessment of a program's merit and worth. Users of the approach might slight quantitative analysis in favor of qualitative analysis. By trying to produce a comprehensive description of a program, the case study evaluator may not produce timely feedback needed to help in program development. To overcome these potential pitfalls, evaluators using the case study approach should fully address the principles of sound evaluation as related to accuracy, utility, feasibility, and propriety.

Approach 13: Criticism and Connoisseurship. The criticism and connoisseur-based approach grew out of methods used in art criticism and literary criticism. It assumes that certain experts in a given substantive area are capable of in-depth analysis and evaluation that could not be done in other ways. Just as a national survey of wine drinkers could produce information concerning their overall preferences for types of wines and particular vineyards, it would not provide the detailed, creditable judgments of the qualities of particular wines that might be derived from a single connoisseur who has devoted a professional lifetime to the study and grading of wines and whose judgments are highly and widely respected.

The advance organizer for the criticism and connoisseur-based study is the evaluator's special expertise and sensitivities. The study's purpose is to describe, critically appraise, and illuminate a particular program's merits. The evaluation questions addressed by the criticism and connoisseur-based evaluation are determined by expert evaluators—the critics and authorities who have undertaken the evaluation. Among the major questions they can be expected to ask are these: What are the program's essence and salient characteristics? What merits and demerits distinguish the particular program from others of the same general kind?

The methodology of criticism and connoisseurship includes critics' systematic use of their perceptual sensitivities, past experiences, refined insights, and abilities to communicate their assessments. The evaluator's judgments are conveyed in vivid terms to help the audience appreciate and understand all of the program's nuances. Eisner (1975, 1983) has pioneered this strategy in education. A dozen or more of Eisner's students have conducted research and development on the criticism and connoisseurship approach, e.g., Vallance (1973) and Flinders and Eisner (2000). This approach obviously depends on the chosen expert's qualifications. It also requires an audience that has confidence in, and is willing to accept and use, the critic/connoisseur's report. I would willingly accept and use any evaluation that Dr. Elliott Eisner agreed to present, but there are not many Eisners out there.

The main advantage of the criticism and connoisseur-based study is that it exploits the particular expertise and finely developed insights of persons who have devoted much time and effort to the study of a precise area. Such individuals can provide an array of detailed information that an audience can then use to form a more insightful analysis than otherwise might be possible. The approach's disadvantage is that it is dependent on the expertise and qualifications of the particular expert doing the program evaluation, leaving room for much subjectivity.

Approach 14: Program Theory-Based Evaluation. Program evaluations based on program theory begin with either (1) a well-developed and validated theory of how programs of a certain type within similar settings operate to produce outcomes or (2) an initial stage to approximate such a theory within the context of a particular program evaluation. The former condition is much more reflective of the implicit promises in a theory-based program evaluation, since the existence of a sound theory means that a substantial body of theoretical development has produced and tested a coherent set of conceptual, hypothetical, and pragmatic principles, as well as associated instruments to guide inquiry. The theory can then aid a program evaluator to decide what questions, indicators, and assumed linkages between and among program elements should be used to evaluate a program covered by the theory.

Some theories have been used more or less successfully to evaluate programs, which gives this approach some measure of viability. For example, health education/behavior change programs are sometimes founded on theoretical frameworks, such as the Health Belief Model (Becker, 1974; Janz and Becker, 1984; Mullen, Hersey, and Iverson, 1987). Other examples are the PRECEDE-PROCEED Model for health promotion planning and evaluation (Green and Kreuter, 1991), Bandura's (1977) Social Cognitive Theory, the Stages of Change Theory of Prochaska and DiClemente (1992), and Peters and Waterman's (1982) theory of successful organizations. When such frameworks exist, their use probably can enhance a program's effectiveness and provide a credible structure for evaluating its functioning. Unfortunately, few program areas are buttressed by well-articulated and tested theories.

Thus, most theory-based evaluations begin by setting out to develop a theory that appropriately could be used to guide the particular program evaluation. As will be discussed later in this characterization, such ad hoc theory development efforts and their linkage to program evaluations are problematic. In any case, let us look at what the theory-based evaluator attempts to achieve.

The point of the theory development or selection effort is to identify advance organizers to guide the evaluation. Essentially, these are the mechanisms by which program activities are understood to produce or contribute to program outcomes, along with the appropriate description of context, specification of independent and dependent variables, and portrayal of key linkages. The main purposes of the theory-based program evaluation are to determine the extent to which the program of interest is theoretically sound, to understand why it is succeeding or failing, and to provide direction for program improvement.

Questions for the program evaluation pertain to and are derived from the guiding theory. Example questions include these: Is the program grounded in an appropriate, well-articulated, and validated theory? Is the employed theory reflective of recent research? Are the program's targeted beneficiaries, design, operation, and intended outcomes consistent with the guiding theory? How well does the program address and serve the full range of pertinent needs of targeted beneficiaries? If the program is consistent with the guiding theory, are the expected results being achieved? Are program inputs and operations producing outcomes in the ways the theory predicts? What changes in the program's design or implementation might produce better outcomes? What elements of the program are essential for successful replication? Overall, was the program theoretically sound, did it operate in accordance with an appropriate theory, did it produce the expected outcomes, were the hypothesized causal linkages confirmed, what program modifications are needed, is the program worthy of continuation and/or dissemination, and what program features are essential for successful replication?

The nature of these questions suggests that the success of the theory-based approach is dependent on a foundation of sound theory development and validation. This, of course, entails sound conceptualization of at least a context-dependent theory, formulation and rigorous testing of hypotheses derived from the theory, development of guidelines for practical implementation of the theory based on extensive field trials, and independent assessment of the theory. Unfortunately, not many program areas in education and the social sciences are grounded in sound theories. Moreover, evaluators wanting to employ a theory-based evaluation do not often find it feasible to conduct the full range of theory development and validation steps and still get the evaluation done effectively and on time. Thus, in claiming to conduct a theory-based evaluation, evaluators often seem to promise much more than they can deliver.

The main procedure typically used in "theory-based program evaluations" is a model of the program's logic. This may be a detailed flowchart of how inputs are thought to be processed to produce intended outcomes. It may also be a grounded theory, such as those advocated by Glaser and Strauss (1967). The network analysis of the former approach is typically an armchair theorizing process involving evaluators and persons who are supposed to know how the program is expected to operate and produce results. They discuss, scheme, discuss some more, network, discuss further, and finally produce networks in varying degrees of detail of what is involved in making the program work and how the various elements are linked to produce desired outcomes. The more demanding grounded theory requires a systematic, empirical process of observing events or analyzing materials drawn from operating programs, followed by an extensive modeling process.

Pioneers in applying theory development procedures to program evaluation include Glaser and Strauss (1967) and Weiss (1972, 1995). Other developers of the approach are Bickman (1990), Chen (1990), and Rogers (2000).

In any program evaluation assignment, it is reasonable for the evaluator to examine the extent to which program plans and operations are grounded in an appropriate theory or model. It can also be useful to engage in a modicum of effort to network the program and thereby seek out key variables and linkages. As noted previously, in the enviable but rare situation where a relevant, validated theory exists, the evaluator can beneficially apply it in structuring the evaluation and in analyzing findings.

However, if a relevant, defensible theory of the program's logic does not exist, evaluators need not develop one. In fact, if they attempt to do so, they will incur many threats to their evaluation's success. Rather than evaluating a program and its underlying logic, evaluators might usurp the program staff's responsibility for program design. They might do a poor job of theory development, given limitations on time and resources to develop and test an appropriate theory. They might incur the conflict of interest associated with having to evaluate the theory they developed. They might pass off an unvalidated model of the program as a theory, when it meets almost none of the requirements of a sound theory. They might bog down the evaluation in too much effort to develop a theory. They might also focus attention on a theory developed early in a program and later discover that the program has evolved to be a quite different enterprise than what was theorized at the outset. In this case, the initial theory could become a "Procrustean bed" for both the program and the program evaluation.

Overall, there really is not much to recommend theory-based program evaluation, since doing it right is usually not feasible and since failed or misrepresented attempts can be highly counterproductive. Nevertheless, modest attempts to model programs—labeled as such—can be useful for identifying measurement variables, so long as the evaluator does not spend too much time on this and so long as the model is not considered as fixed or as a validated theory. In the rare case where an appropriate theory already exists, the evaluator can make beneficial use of it to help structure and guide the evaluation and interpret the findings.

Approach 15: Mixed-Methods Studies.   In an attempt to resolve the longstanding debate about whether program evaluations should employ quantitative or qualitative methods, some authors have proposed that evaluators should regularly combine these methods in given program evaluations (for example, see the National Science Foundation's 1997 *User-Friendly Handbook for Mixed Method Evaluations*). Such recommendations, along with practical guidelines and illustrations, are no doubt useful to many program staff members and to evaluators. But in the main, the recommendation for a mixed-methods approach only highlights a large body of longstanding practice of mixed-methods program evaluation rather than proposing a new approach. All seven approaches discussed in the remainder of this section of the monograph employ both qualitative and quantitative methods. What sets them apart from the mixed-methods approach is that their first considerations are not the methods to be employed but either the assessment of value or the social mission to be served. The mixed-methods approach is included in this section on questions/methods approaches, because it is preoccupied with using multiple methods rather than whatever methods are needed to comprehensively assess a program's merit and worth. As with the other approaches in this section, the mixed-methods approach may or may not fully assess a program's value; thus, it is classified as a quasi-evaluation approach.

The advance organizers of the mixed-methods approach are formative and summative evaluations, qualitative and quantitative methods, and intracase or cross-case analysis. Formative evaluations are employed to examine a program's development and assist in improving its structure and implementation. Summative evaluations basically look at whether objectives were achieved, but may look for a broader array of outcomes. Qualitative and quantitative methods are employed in combination to assure depth, scope, and dependability of findings. This approach also applies to carefully selected single programs or to comparisons of alternative programs.

The basic purposes of the mixed methods approach are to provide direction for improving programs as they evolve and to assess their effectiveness after they have had time to produce results. Use of both quantitative and qualitative methods is intended to ensure dependable feedback on a wide range of questions; depth of understanding of particular programs; a holistic perspective; and enhancement of the validity, reliability, and usefulness of the full set of findings. Investigators look to quantitative methods for standardized, replicable findings on large data sets. They look to qualitative methods for elucidation of the program's cultural context, dynamics, meaningful patterns and themes, deviant cases, and diverse impacts on individuals as well as groups. Qualitative reporting methods are applied to bring the findings to life, to make them clear, persuasive, and interesting. By using both quantitative and qualitative methods, the evaluator secures crosschecks on different subsets of findings and thereby instills greater stakeholder confidence in the overall findings.

The sources of evaluation questions are the program's goals, plans, and stakeholders. The stakeholders often include skeptical as well as supportive audiences. Among the important stakeholders are program administrators and staff, policy boards, financial sponsors, beneficiaries, citizens, and program area experts.

The approach may pursue a wide range of questions. Examples of formative evaluation questions follow: To what extent do program activities follow the program plan, time line, and budget? To what extent is the program achieving its goals? What problems in design or implementation need to be addressed? Examples of summative evaluation questions are, To what extent did the program achieve its goals? Was the program appropriately effective for all beneficiaries? What interesting stories emerged? What are program stakeholders' judgments of program operations, processes, and outcomes? What were the important side effects? Is the program sustainable and transportable?

The approach employs a wide range of methods. Among quantitative methods are surveys using representative samples, and both cohort and cross-sectional samples, norm-referenced tests, rating scales, quasi experiments, significance tests for main effects, and a posteriori statistical tests. The qualitative methods may include ethnography, document analysis, narrative analysis, purposive samples, participant observers, independent observers, key informants, advisory committees, structured and unstructured interviews, focus groups, case studies of individuals and groups, study of outliers, diaries, logic models, grounded theory development, flow charts, decision trees, matrices, and performance assessments. Reports may include abstracts, executive summaries, full reports, oral briefings, conference presentations, and workshops. They should include a balance of narrative and numerical information.

Considering his book on service studies in higher education, Ralph Tyler (Tyler et al., 1932) was certainly a pioneer in the mixed-methods approach to program evaluation. Other authors who have written cogently on the approach are Guba and Lincoln (1981), Kidder and Fine (1987), Lincoln and Guba (1985), Miron (1998), Patton (1990), and Schatzman and Strauss (1973).

It is almost always appropriate to consider using a mixed-methods approach. Certainly, the evaluator should take advantage of opportunities to obtain any and all potentially available information that is relevant to assessing a program's merit and worth. Sometimes a study can be mainly or only qualitative or quantitative. But usually such studies would be strengthened by including both types of information. The key point is to choose methods because they can effectively address the study's questions, not because they are either qualitative or quantitative.

Key advantages of using both qualitative and quantitative methods are that they complement each other in ways that are important to the evaluation's audiences. Information from quantitative methods tends to be standardized, efficient, and amenable to standard tests of reliability, easily summarized and analyzed, and accepted as hard data. Information from qualitative approaches adds depth; can be delivered in interesting, story-like presentations; and provides a means to explore and understand the more superficial quantitative findings. Using both types of method affords important crosschecks on findings.

The main pitfall in pursuing the mixed-methods approach is using multiple methods because this is the popular thing to do rather than because the selected methods best respond to the evaluation questions. Moreover, sometimes evaluators let the combination of methods compensate for a lack of rigor in applying them. Using a mixed-methods approach can produce confusing findings if an investigator uncritically mixes positivistic and postmodern paradigms, since quantitative and qualitative methods are derived from different theoretical approaches to inquiry and reflect different conceptions of knowledge. Many evaluators do not possess the requisite foundational knowledge in both the sciences and humanities to effectively combine quantitative and qualitative methods. The approaches in the remainder of this monograph place proper emphasis on mixed methods, making choice of the methods subservient to the approach's dominant philosophy and to the particular evaluation questions to be addressed.

The mixed-methods approach to evaluation concludes this monograph's discussion of the questions/methods approaches to evaluation. These 13 approaches tend to concentrate on selected questions and methods and thus may or may not fully address an evaluation's fundamental requirement to assess a program's merit and worth. The array of these approaches suggests that the field has advanced considerably since the 1950s when program evaluations were rare and mainly used approaches grounded in behavioral objectives, standardized tests, and/or accreditation visits.

Tables 1 through 6 summarize the similarities and differences among the models in relationship to advance organizers, purposes, characteristic questions, methods, strengths, and weaknesses.

Improvement/Accountability-Oriented Evaluation Approaches

I now turn to three approaches that stress the need to fully assess a program's merit and worth. These approaches are expansive and seek comprehensiveness in considering the full range of questions and criteria needed to assess a program's value. Often they employ the assessed needs of a program's stakeholders as the foundational criteria for assessing the program's merit and worth. They also seek to examine the full range of pertinent technical and economic criteria for judging program plans and operations. They look for all relevant outcomes, not just those keyed to program objectives. Usually, they are objectivist and assume an underlying reality in seeking definitive, unequivocal answers to the evaluation questions. Typically, they must use multiple qualitative and quantitative assessment methods to provide crosschecks on findings. In general, the approaches conform closely to this monograph's definition of evaluation. The approaches are labeled Decision/Accountability, Consumer-Orientation, and Accreditation. The three approaches respectively emphasize improvement through serving program decisions, providing consumers with assessments of optional programs and services, and helping consumers to examine the merits of competing institutions and programs.

Approach 16: Decision/Accountability-Oriented Studies. The decision/accountability-oriented approach emphasizes that program evaluation should be used proactively to help improve a program as well as retroactively to judge its merit and worth. The approach is distinguished from management information systems and from politically controlled studies because decision/accountability-oriented studies emphasize questions of merit and worth. The approach's philosophical underpinnings

Table 1: Comparison of the 13 Questions and Methods Oriented Evaluation Approaches on Most Common ADVANCE ORGANIZERS

Advance Organizers	Evaluation Approaches (by identification number)*												
	3	4	5	6	7	8	9	10	11	12	13	14	15
Program content/definition		✓								✓			
Program rationale										✓			
Context												✓	
Treatments						✓							
Time period										✓			
Beneficiaries										✓			
Comparison groups						✓							
Norm groups			✓										
Assessed needs										✓			
Problem statements						✓							
Objectives	✓	✓	✓		✓								
Independent/dependent variables						✓						✓	
Indicators/criteria				✓					✓				
Life skills					✓								
Performance tasks					✓								
Questions/hypotheses/causal factors						✓						✓	
Policy issues				✓									
Tests in use		✓	✓										
Formative & summative evaluation													✓
Qualitative & quantitative methods													✓
Program activities/milestones							✓						
Employee roles & responsibilities		✓								✓			
Costs								✓					
Evaluator expertise & sensitivities											✓		
Intra-case/cross-case analysis													✓

* 3. Objectives-based, 4. Accountability, 5. Objective testing, 6. Outcome/value-added assessment, 7. Performance testing, 8. Experiments, 9. Management information systems, 10. Benefit-cost analysis, 11. Clarification hearing, 12. Case study, 13. Criticism & connoisseurship, 14. Program theory-based, 15. Mixed methods.

Table 2: Comparison of the 13 Questions and Methods Oriented Evaluation Approaches on Primary EVALUATION PURPOSES

Evaluation Purposes	*Evaluation Approaches (by identification number)**												
	3	4	5	6	7	8	9	10	11	12	13	14	15
Determine whether program objectives were achieved	✓				✓		✓	✓					✓
Provide constituents with an accurate accounting of results		✓		✓	✓	✓			✓				
Assure that results are positive		✓											
Assess learning gains				✓									
Pinpoint responsibility for good & bad outcomes		✓		✓	✓								
Compare students' test scores to norms			✓										
Compare students' test performance to standards	✓		✓		✓								
Diagnose program shortcomings		✓	✓				✓		✓		✓		
Compare performance of competing programs		✓	✓	✓	✓		✓						
Examine achievement trends		✓	✓										
Inform policymaking		✓		✓	✓	✓							
Direction for program improvement					✓		✓					✓	✓
Ensure standardization of outcome measures		✓		✓									
Determine cause and effect relationships in programs						✓					✓		
Inform management decisions & actions							✓						
Assess investments and payoffs								✓					
Provide balanced information on strengths & weaknesses										✓			✓
Explicate & illuminate a program										✓	✓		
Describe & critically appraise a program											✓		
Assess a program's theoretical soundness												✓	

* 3. Objectives-based, 4. Accountability, 5. Objective testing, 6. Outcome/value-added assessment, 7. Performance testing, 8. Experiments, 9. Management information systems, 10. Benefit-cost analysis, 11. Clarification hearing, 12. Case study, 13. Criticism & connoisseurship, 14. Program theory-based, 15. Mixed methods.

Table 3: Comparison of the 13 Questions and Methods Oriented Evaluation Approaches on Characteristic EVALUATION QUESTIONS

Evaluation Questions	Evaluation Approaches (by identification number)*												
	3	4	5	6	7	8	9	10	11	12	13	14	15
To what extent was each program objective achieved?	✓											✓	✓
Did the program effectively discharge its responsibilities?		✓											✓
Did tested performance meet or exceed pertinent norms?			✓										
Did tested performance meet or exceed standards?	✓		✓										
Where does a group's tested performance rank compared with other groups?	✓	✓											
Is a group's present performance better than past performance?	✓	✓	✓										
What sectors of a system are performing best and poorest?				✓									
Where are the shortfalls in specific curricular areas?				✓									
At what grade levels are the strengths & shortfalls?				✓									
What value is being added by particular programs?				✓									
To what extent can students effectively speak, write, figure, analyze, lead, work cooperatively, & solve problems?					✓								
What are a program's effects on outcomes?						✓						✓	
Are program activities being implemented according to schedule, budget, & expected results?							✓						
What is the program's return on investment?								✓					

Table 3 (*continued*)

Evaluation Questions	Evaluation Approaches (by identification number)*												
	3	4	5	6	7	8	9	10	11	12	13	14	15
Is the program sustainable & transportable?							✓	✓					✓
Is the program worthy of continuation and/or dissemination?		✓				✓		✓	✓		✓		
Is the program as good or better than others that address the same objectives?						✓			✓		✓		
What is the program in concept & practice?										✓		✓	
How has the program evolved over time?										✓			
How does the program produce outcomes?										✓		✓	
What has the program produced?										✓		✓	
What are the program's shortfalls & negative side effects?										✓			✓
What are the program's positive side effects?										✓			✓
How do various stakeholders value the program?										✓			✓
Did the program meet all the beneficiaries' needs?										✓		✓	✓
What were the most important reasons for the program's success or failure?										✓		✓	
What are the program's most important unresolved issues?										✓			
How much did the program cost?								✓		✓			
What were the costs per beneficiary, per year, etc.?								✓		✓			
What parts of the program were successfully transported to other sites?										✓			
What are the program's essence & salient characteristics?										✓	✓		

Table 3 (*continued*)

Evaluation Questions	Evaluation Approaches (by identification number)*												
	3	4	5	6	7	8	9	10	11	12	13	14	15
What merits & demerits distinguish the program from similar programs?										✓	✓		
Is the program grounded in a validated theory?												✓	
Are program operations consistent with the guiding theory?												✓	
Were hypothesized causal linkages confirmed?						✓						✓	
What changes in the program's design or implementation might produce better outcomes?	✓					✓			✓	✓	✓	✓	✓
What program features are essential for successful replication?									✓	✓	✓		
What interesting stories emerged?										✓			✓

* 3. Objectives-based, 4. Accountability, 5. Objective testing, 6. Outcome/value-added assessment, 7. Performance testing, 8. Experiments, 9. Management information systems, 10. Benefit-cost analysis, 11. Clarification hearing, 12. Case study, 13. Criticism & connoisseurship, 14. Program theory-based, 15. Mixed methods.

Table 4: Comparison of the 13 Questions and Methods Oriented Evaluation Approaches on Main EVALUATION METHODS

Evaluation Methods	Evaluation Approaches (by identification number)*												
	3	4	5	6	7	8	9	10	11	12	13	14	15
Operational objectives	✓												✓
Criterion-referenced tests	✓				✓					✓			✓
Performance contracting		✓											
Program Planning & Budgeting System		✓					✓						
Program Evaluation & Review Technique							✓						
Management by objectives	✓	✓					✓						
Staff progress reports							✓						
Financial reports & audits							✓						
Zero Based Budgeting		✓											
Cost analysis, cost-effectiveness analysis, & benefit-cost analysis								✓					
Mandated "program drivers" & indicators		✓											
Input, process, output databases		✓					✓						
Independent goal achievement auditors	✓	✓											
Procedural compliance audits		✓											
Peer review		✓											
Merit pay for individuals and/or organizations		✓											
Collective bargaining agreements		✓											
Trial proceedings									✓				
Mandated testing		✓										✓	
Institutional report cards		✓											
Self-studies		✓											
Site visits by experts		✓											
Program audits		✓											
Standardized testing			✓	✓						✓			✓
Performance measures					✓					✓			✓
Computerized or other database				✓			✓			✓			
Hierarchical mixed model analysis				✓									
Policy analysis				✓									
Experimental & quasi-experimental designs						✓							✓

Table 4 (*continued*)

Evaluation Methods	Evaluation Approaches (by identification number)*												
	3	4	5	6	7	8	9	10	11	12	13	14	15
Study of outliers						✓				✓			✓
System analysis							✓						
Analysis of archives										✓			✓
Collection of artifacts										✓			✓
Log diaries													✓
Content analysis										✓			✓
Independent & participant observers										✓			✓
Key informants										✓			✓
Advisory committees													✓
Interviews										✓			✓
Operations analysis										✓			
Focus groups										✓			✓
Questionnaires										✓			✓
Rating scales										✓			✓
Hearings & forums									✓	✓			
In-depth descriptions										✓			
Photographs										✓			
Critical incidents										✓			
Testimony									✓	✓			✓
Flow charts													✓
Decision trees													✓
Logic models										✓		✓	✓
Grounded theory												✓	✓
News clippings analysis										✓			✓
Cross-break tables	✓			✓						✓			✓
Expert critics									✓	✓	✓		✓

* 3. Objectives-based, 4. Accountability, 5. Objective testing, 6. Outcome/value-added assessment, 7. Performance testing, 8. Experiments, 9. Management information systems, 10. Benefit-cost analysis, 11. Clarification hearing, 12. Case study, 13. Criticism & connoisseurship, 14. Program theory-based, 15. Mixed methods.

Table 5: Comparison of the 13 Questions and Methods Oriented Evaluation Approaches on Prevalent STRENGTHS

Strengths	Evaluation Approaches (by identification number)*												
	3	4	5	6	7	8	9	10	11	12	13	14	15
Common sense appeal	✓			✓	✓	✓		✓	✓				✓
Widely known & applied	✓		✓			✓							✓
Employs operational objectives	✓												
Employs the technology of testing	✓			✓	✓	✓	✓						✓
Efficient use of standardized tests				✓	✓								
Popular among constituents & politicians			✓	✓	✓		✓						
Focus on improving public services	✓												
Can focus on audience's most important questions							✓		✓	✓			✓
Defines obligations of service providers	✓												
Requires production of and reporting on positive outcomes	✓												
Seeks to improve services through competition	✓					✓							
Efficient means of data collection			✓	✓			✓						
Stress on validity & reliability			✓	✓		✓							✓
Triangulates findings from multiple sources									✓	✓			✓
Uses institutionalized database				✓									
Monitors progress on each student			✓	✓									
Emphasizes service to every student				✓									
Hierarchical analysis of achievement				✓									
Conducive to policy analysis				✓		✓							
Employs trend analysis				✓									
Strong provision for analyzing qualitative information					✓					✓	✓		
Rejects use of artificial cut scores					✓					✓			

Table 5 (*continued*)

Strengths	Evaluation Approaches (by identification number)*												
	3	4	5	6	7	8	9	10	11	12	13	14	15
Considers student background by using students as their own controls				✓									
Considers contextual influences				✓						✓			✓
Uses authentic measures					✓								✓
Eliminates guessing					✓								
Reinforces life skills					✓								
Focuses on outcomes	✓	✓	✓	✓	✓	✓							✓
Focuses on a program's strengths & weaknesses		✓							✓				✓
Determines cause & effects						✓							
Examines program's internal workings & how it produces outcomes										✓	✓		
Guides program management							✓						
Helps keep programs on track							✓						
Guides broad study & improvement of program processes & outcomes							✓						✓
Can be done retrospectively or in real time										✓	✓	✓	✓
Documents costs of program inputs								✓					
Maintains a financial history for the program								✓					
Contrasts program alternatives on both costs & outcomes								✓					
Employs rules of evidence									✓				
Requires no controls of treatments & participants										✓	✓		
Examines programs as they naturally occur										✓	✓		
Examines programs holistically & in depth										✓	✓		

Table 5 (*continued*)

Strengths	Evaluation Approaches (by identification number)*												
	3	4	5	6	7	8	9	10	11	12	13	14	15
Engages experts to render refined descriptions & judgments										✓	✓		
Yields in-depth, refined, effectively communi- cated analysis										✓	✓		
Employs all relevant information sources & methods										✓			✓
Stresses complementarity of qualitative & quan- titative methods										✓			✓

* 3. Objectives-based, 4. Accountability, 5. Objective testing, 6. Outcome/value-added assessment, 7. Performance testing, 8. Experiments, 9. Management information systems, 10. Benefit-cost analysis, 11. Clarification hearing, 12. Case study, 13. Criticism & connoisseurship, 14. Program theory-based, 15. Mixed methods.

Table 6: Comparison of the 13 Questions and Methods Oriented Evaluation Approaches on Prevalent WEAKNESSES/LIMITATIONS

Weaknesses/Limitations	*Evaluation Approaches (by identification number)**												
	3	4	5	6	7	8	9	10	11	12	13	14	15
May credit unworthy objectives	✓												
May define a program's success in terms that are too narrow and mechanical and not attuned to beneficiaries' various needs							✓						
May employ only lower-order learning objectives	✓		✓	✓									
Relies almost exclusively on multiple choice test data			✓	✓									
May indicate mainly socio-economic status, not quality of teaching & learning				✓									
May reinforce & over-emphasize multiple choice test taking ability to the exclusion of writing, speaking, etc.			✓	✓									
May poorly test what teachers teach			✓	✓									
Yields mainly terminal information that lacks utility for program improvement	✓						✓						
Provides data only on student outcomes	✓		✓	✓	✓								
Narrow scope of skills that can feasibly be assessed					✓								
May provide too narrow an information basis for judging a program's merit & worth	✓		✓	✓	✓	✓	✓	✓			✓		
May employ many methods because it is the thing to do rather than because they are needed												✓	
May inappropriately & counterproductively mix positivistic & post-modern paradigms												✓	

Table 6 (*continued*)

Weaknesses/Limitations	Evaluation Approaches (by identification number)*												
	3	4	5	6	7	8	9	10	11	12	13	14	15
May oversimplify the complexities involved in assigning responsibility for student learning gains to individual teachers				✓									
May miss important side effects	✓		✓	✓	✓	✓							
May rely too heavily on the expertise & judgment of a single evaluator											✓		
May issue invidious comparisons		✓	✓	✓	✓								
May produce unhealthy competition		✓	✓	✓	✓				✓				
May provoke political unrest		✓	✓	✓	✓				✓				
Accuracy suffers in the face of competing evaluations									✓				
May undesirably narrow the range of program services		✓										✓	
Politicians tend to press for premature implementation		✓	✓		✓								
Granting rewards & sanctions may produce cheating		✓	✓		✓								
Inordinate time requirements for administration & scoring					✓								
High costs of scoring					✓								
Difficulty in achieving reliability					✓								
High cost					✓								
Low feasibility				✓	✓		✓						
May inappropriately deprive control group subjects of entitlements						✓							
Carries a connotation of experimenting on children or other subjects using unproven methods						✓							

Table 6 (*continued*)

Weaknesses/Limitations	Evaluation Approaches (by identification number)*												
	3	4	5	6	7	8	9	10	11	12	13	14	15
Requirement of random assignment is often not feasible						✓							
Tend to stifle continual improvement of the program						✓							
Vital data may be inaccessible to evaluators							✓						
Investigators may mistake the approach's openness & lack of controls as license to ignore rigor										✓			
Evaluators might usurp the program staff's responsibility for program design												✓	
Might ground an evaluation in a hastily developed, inadequate program theory												✓	
Might develop a conflict of interest to defend the evaluation-generated program theory												✓	
Might bog down the evaluation in a seemingly endless process of program theory development												✓	
Might create a theory early in a program and impede the program from redefinition and refinement												✓	

* 3. Objectives-based, 4. Accountability, 5. Objective testing, 6. Outcome/value-added assessment, 7. Performance testing, 8. Experiments, 9. Management information systems, 10. Benefit-cost analysis, 11. Clarification hearing, 12. Case study, 13. Criticism & connoisseurship, 14. Program theory-based, 15. Mixed methods.

include an objectivist orientation to finding best answers to context-limited questions and subscription to the principles of a well-functioning democratic society, especially human rights, equity, excellence, conservation, and accountability. Practically, the approach engages stakeholders in focusing the evaluation; addressing their most important questions; providing timely, relevant information to assist decision making; and producing an accountability record.

The advance organizers for the approach include decision makers/ stakeholders, projected decision situations, and program accountability requirements. Audiences include not just top managers but stakeholders at all organizational program levels. From the bottom up, such stakeholders may include beneficiaries, parents/guardians, service providers, administrators, program consultants, support personnel, policymakers, funding authorities, and citizens. The generic decision situations to be served may include defining goals and priorities, choosing from competing services, planning programs, budgeting, staffing, using services, guiding participation, judging progress, and recycling program operations. Key classes of needed evaluative information are assessments of needs, problems, and opportunities; identification and assessment of competing programs or program approaches; assessment of program plans; assessment of staff qualifications and performance; assessment of program facilities and materials; monitoring and assessment of process; assessment of intended and unintended and short-range and long-range outcomes; and assessment of cost-effectiveness.

The basic purpose of decision/accountability studies is to provide a knowledge and value base for making and being accountable for decisions that result in developing, delivering, and making informed use of cost-effective services. Thus, evaluators must interact with representative members of their audiences; discern their questions; and supply them with relevant, timely, efficient, and accurate information. The approach stresses that an evaluation's most important purpose is not to prove but to improve.

The sources of questions addressed by this approach are the concerned and involved stakeholders. These may include all persons and groups who must make choices related to initiating, planning, funding, implementing, and using a program's services. Main questions addressed are, Has an appropriate beneficiary population been determined? What beneficiary needs should be addressed? What are the available alternative ways to address these needs, and what are their comparative merits and costs? Are plans of services and participation sound? Is there adequate provision for facilities, materials, and equipment? Is the program staff sufficiently qualified and credible? Have appropriate roles been assigned to the different participants? Are the participants effectively carrying out their assignments? Is the program working and should it be revised in any way? Is the program effectively reaching all the targeted beneficiaries? Is the program meeting the participants' needs? Did beneficiaries play their part? Is the program better than competing alternatives? Is it affordable? Is it sustainable? Is it transportable? Is the program worth the required initial investment? Answers to these and related questions are to be based on the underlying standard of good programs, i.e., they must reach and serve beneficiaries' targeted needs effectively at a reasonable cost and do so as well as or better than reasonably available alternatives.

Many methods may be used in decision/accountability-oriented program evaluations. These include, among others, surveys, needs assessments, case studies, advocate teams, observations, interviews, resident evaluators, and quasi-experimental and experimental designs. To make the approach work, the evaluator must regularly interact with a representative body of stakeholders. Typically, the evaluator should establish and engage a representative stakeholder advisory panel to help define evaluation questions, shape evaluation plans, review draft reports, and help disseminate findings. The evaluator's exchanges with this group involve conveying evaluation feedback that may be of use in program improvement and use, as well as determining what future evaluation reports would be most helpful to program personnel and other stakeholders. Interim reports may assist beneficiaries, program staff, and others to obtain feedback on the program's merits and worth, as well as on the quality of their participation. By maintaining a dynamic baseline of evaluation information and applications of the information, the evaluator can use this information to develop a comprehensive summative evaluation report, periodically update the broad group of stakeholders, and supply program personnel with findings for their own accountability reports.

The involvement of stakeholders is consistent with a key principle of the change process. An enterprise—read *evaluation* here—can best help bring about change in a target group's behavior if that group was involved in planning, monitoring, and judging the enterprise. By involving stakeholders throughout the evaluation process, decision-oriented evaluators lay the groundwork for bringing stakeholders to understand and value the evaluation process and apply the findings.

Cronbach (1963) advised educators to reorient their evaluations from an objectives orientation to a concern for making better program decisions. While he did not use the terms *formative* and *summative* evaluation, he essentially defined the underlying concepts. In discussing the distinctions between the constructive, proactive orientation on the one hand and the retrospective, judgmental orientation on the other, he argued for placing more emphasis on the former. He noted the limited functionality of the tradition of stressing retrospective outcomes evaluation. Later, I (Stufflebeam, 1966, 1967) argued that evaluations should help program personnel make and defend decisions keyed to meeting beneficiaries' needs. While I advocated an improvement orientation to evaluation, I also emphasized that evaluators must both inform decisions and provide information for accountability. I also emphasized that the approach should interact with and serve the full range of stakeholders who need to make judgments and choices about a program. Others who have contributed to the development of a decision/accountability orientation to evaluation are Alkin (1969) and Webster (1975, 1995).

The decision/accountability-oriented approach is applicable in cases where program staff and other stakeholders want and need both formative and summative evaluation. It can provide the evaluation framework for both internal and external evaluation. When used for internal evaluation, it is often advisable to commission an independent metaevaluation of the inside evaluator's work. Beyond program evaluations, this approach has proved useful in evaluating personnel, students, projects, facilities, and products.

A major advantage of the approach is that it encourages program personnel to use evaluation continuously and systematically to plan and implement programs that meet beneficiaries' targeted needs. It aids decision making at all program levels and stresses improvement. It also presents a rationale and framework of information for helping program personnel be accountable for their program decisions and actions. It involves the full range of stakeholders in the evaluation process to ensure that their evaluation needs are well addressed and to encourage and support them to make effective use of evaluation findings. It is comprehensive in attending to context, inputs, process, and outcomes. It balances the use of quantitative and qualitative methods. It is keyed to professional standards for evaluations. Finally, the approach emphasizes that evaluations must be grounded in the democratic principles of a free society.

A major limitation is that the collaboration required between an evaluator and stakeholders introduces opportunities for impeding the evaluation and/or biasing its results, especially when the evaluative situation is politically charged. Further, when evaluators are actively influencing a program's course, they may identify so closely with it that they lose some of the independent, detached perspective needed to provide objective, forthright reports. Moreover, the approach may overemphasize formative evaluation and give too little time and resources to summative evaluation. External metaevaluation has been employed to counteract opportunities for bias and to ensure a proper balance of the formative and summative aspects of evaluation. Though the charge is erroneous, this approach carries the connotation that only top decision makers are served.

Approach 17: Consumer-Oriented Studies. In the consumer-oriented approach, the evaluator is the enlightened surrogate consumer. He or she must draw direct evaluative conclusions about the program being evaluated. Evaluation is viewed as the process of determining something's merit and worth, with evaluations being the products of that process. The approach regards a consumer's welfare as a program's primary justification and accords that welfare the same primacy in program evaluation. Grounded in a deeply reasoned view of ethics and the common good, together with skills in obtaining and synthesizing pertinent, valid, and reliable information, the evaluator should help developers produce and deliver products and services that are of excellent quality and of great use to consumers (for example, students, their parents, teachers, and taxpayers). More importantly, the evaluator should help consumers identify and assess the merit and worth of competing programs, services, and products.

Advance organizers include societal values, consumers' needs, costs, and criteria of goodness in the particular evaluation domain. The purpose of a consumer-oriented program evaluation is to judge the relative merits and worth of the products and services of alternative programs and thereby to help taxpayers, practitioners, and potential beneficiaries make wise choices. The approach is objectivist in assuming an underlying reality and positing that it is possible, although often extremely difficult, to find best answers. It looks at a program comprehensively in terms of its quality and costs, functionally regarding the assessed needs of the intended beneficiaries, and comparatively considering reasonably available alternative programs. Evaluators are expected to subject their program evaluations to evaluations, what Scriven has termed *metaevaluation*.

The approach employs a wide range of assessment topics. These include program description, background and context, client, consumers, resources, function, delivery system, values, standards, process, outcomes, costs, critical competitors, generalizability, statistical significance, assessed needs, bottom-line assessment, practical significance, recommendations, reports, and metaevaluation. The evaluation process begins with consideration of a broad range of such topics, continuously compiles information on all of them, and ultimately culminates in a super-compressed judgment of the program's merit and worth.

Questions for the consumer-oriented study are derived from society, from program constituents, and especially from the evaluator's frame of reference. One general question is addressed: Which of several alternative programs is the best choice, given their differential costs, the needs of the consumer group, the values of society at large, and evidence of both positive and negative outcomes?

Methods include checklists, needs assessments, goal-free evaluation, experimental and quasi-experimental designs, modus operandi analysis, applying codes of ethical conduct, and cost analysis (Scriven, 1974). A preferred method is for an external, independent consumer advocate to conduct and report findings of studies of publicly supported programs. The approach is keyed to employing a sound checklist of the program's key aspects. Scriven (1991) developed a generic "Key Evaluation Checklist" for this purpose. This and other checklists are available on the following Web page <www.wmich.edu/evalctr/checklists>. The main evaluative acts in this approach are scoring, grading, ranking, apportioning, and producing the final synthesis (Scriven, 1994a).

Scriven (1967) was a pioneer in applying the consumer-oriented approach to program evaluation, and his work parallels the concurrent work of Ralph Nader and the Consumers Union in the general field of consumerism. Glass (1975) has supported and developed Scriven's approach. Scriven coined the terms *formative* and *summative* evaluation. He allowed that evaluations can be divergent in early quests for critical competitors and explorations related to clarifying goals and making programs function well. However, he also maintained that ultimately evaluations must converge on summative judgments about a program's merit and worth. While accepting the importance of formative evaluation, he also argued against Cronbach's (1963) position that formative evaluation should be given the major emphasis. According to Scriven, the fundamental aim of a sound evaluation is to judge a program's merit, comparative value, and overall worth. He sees evaluation as a transdiscipline encompassing all evaluations of various entities across all applied areas and disciplines and comprised of a common logic, methodology, and theory that transcends specific evaluation domains, which also have their unique characteristics (Scriven, 1991, 1994a).

The consumer-oriented study requires a highly credible and competent expert, together with either sufficient resources to allow the expert to conduct a thorough study or other means to obtain the needed information. Often, a consumer-oriented evaluator is engaged to evaluate a program after its formative stages are over. In these situations, the external consumer-oriented evaluator is often dependent on being able to access a substantial base of information that the program staff had accumulated. If no such base of information exists, the consumer-oriented evaluator will have great difficulty in obtaining enough information to produce a thorough, defensible summative program evaluation.

One of the main advantages of consumer-oriented evaluation is that it is a hard-hitting, independent assessment intended to protect consumers from shoddy programs, services, and products and to guide them to support and use those contributions that best and most cost-effectively address their needs. The approach's stress on independent/objective assessment and its attempt to achieve a comprehensive assessment of merit and worth yield high credibility with consumer groups. This is aided by Michael Scriven's (1991) Key Evaluation Checklist and his *Evaluation Thesaurus* (in which he presents and explains the checklist). The approach provides for a summative evaluation to yield a bottom-line judgment of merit and worth, preceded by a formative evaluation to assist developers to help ensure that their programs will succeed.

One disadvantage of the consumer-oriented evaluation is that it can be so independent from practitioners that it may not assist them to better serve consumers. If a summative evaluation is conducted too early, it can intimidate developers and stifle their creativity. However, if the summative evaluation is applied only near a program's end, the evaluator may have great difficulty in obtaining sufficient evidence to confidently and credibly judge the program's basic value. This often iconoclastic approach is also heavily dependent on a highly competent, independent, and "bulletproof" evaluator.

Approach 18: Accreditation/Certification Approach. Many educational institutions, hospitals, and other service organizations have periodically been the subject of an accreditation study; and many professionals, at one time or another, have had to meet certification requirements for a given position. Such studies of institutions and personnel are in the realm of accountability-oriented evaluations, as well as having an improvement element. Institutions, institutional programs, and personnel are studied to prove whether they meet requirements of given professions and service areas and whether they are fit to serve designated functions in society; typically, the feedback reports identify areas for improvement.

The advance organizers used in the accreditation/certification study usually are guidelines and criteria that some accrediting or certifying body has adopted. As previously suggested, the evaluation's purpose is to determine whether institutions, institutional programs, and/or personnel should be approved to deliver specified public services.

The source of questions for accreditation or certification studies is the accrediting or certifying body. Basically, they address these questions: Are institutions and their programs and personnel meeting minimum standards, and how can their performance be improved?

Typical methods used in the accreditation/certification approach are self-study and self-reporting by the individual or institution. In the case of institutions, panels of experts are assigned to visit the institution, verify a self-report, and gather additional information. The basis for the self-studies and the visits by expert panels are usually guidelines and criteria that have been specified by the accrediting agency.

Accreditation of education was pioneered by the College Entrance Examination Board around 1901. Since then, the accreditation function has been implemented and expanded, especially by the Cooperative Study of Secondary School Standards, dating from around 1933. Subsequently, the accreditation approach has been developed, further expanded, and administered by the North Central Association of Secondary Schools and Colleges, along with its associated regional accrediting agencies across the United States, and by many other accrediting and certifying bodies. Similar accreditation practices are found in medicine, law, architecture, and many other professions.

Any area of professional service that potentially could put the public at risk if services are not delivered by highly trained specialists in accordance with standards of good practice and safety should consider subjecting its programs to accreditation reviews and its personnel to certification processes. Such use of evaluation services is very much in the public interest and is also a means of getting feedback that can be of use in strengthening capabilities and practices.

The major advantage of the accreditation or certification study is that it aids lay persons in making informed judgments about the quality of organizations and programs and the qualifications of individual personnel.

Major difficulties are that the guidelines of accrediting and certifying bodies often emphasize inputs and processes and not outcomes. Further, the self-study and visitation processes used in accreditation offer many opportunities for corruption and inept performance. As is the case for a number of the evaluation approaches described above, it is prudent to subject accreditation and certification processes themselves to independent meta-evaluations.

The three improvement/accountability-oriented approaches emphasize the assessment of merit and worth, which is the thrust of the definition of evaluation used to classify the twenty-two approaches considered in this monograph. Tables 7 through 12 summarize the similarities and differences among the models in relationship to advance organizers, purposes, characteristic questions, methods, strengths, and weaknesses. The monograph turns next to the fourth and final set of program evaluation approaches—those concerned with using evaluation to further some social agenda.

Social Agenda/Advocacy Approaches

Social Agenda/Advocacy approaches are directed to making a difference in society through program evaluation. These approaches seek to ensure that all segments of society have equal access to educational and social opportunities and services. They have an affirmative action bent toward giving preferential treatment through program evaluation to the disadvantaged. If—as many persons have stated—information is power, then these approaches employ program evaluation to empower the disenfranchised.

The four approaches in this set are oriented to employing the perspectives of stakeholders as well as of experts in characterizing, investigating, and judging programs. They favor a constructivist orientation and the use of qualitative methods. For the most part, they eschew the possibility of finding right or best answers and reflect the philosophy of postmodernism, with its attendant stress on cultural pluralism, moral relativity, and multiple realities. They provide for democratic engagement of stakeholders in obtaining and interpreting findings.

There is a concern that these approaches might concentrate so heavily on serving a social mission that they fail to meet the standards of a sound evaluation. By giving stakeholders the authority for key evaluation decisions, related especially to interpretation and release of findings, evaluators empower these persons to use evaluation to their best advantage. Such delegation of authority over important evaluation matters makes the evaluation vulnerable to bias and other misuse. Further, if an evaluator is intent on serving the underprivileged, empowering the disenfranchised, and/or righting educational and/or social injustices, he or she might compromise the independent, impartial perspective needed to produce valid findings, especially if funds allocated to serve these groups would be withdrawn as a consequence of a negative report. In the extreme, an advocacy evaluation could compromise the integrity of the evaluation process to achieve social objectives and thus devolve into a pseudoevaluation.

Nevertheless, there is much to recommend these approaches, since they are strongly oriented to democratic principles of equity and fairness and employ practical procedures for involving the full range of stakeholders. The particular social agenda/advocacy approaches presented in this monograph seem to have sufficient safeguards needed to walk the line between sound evaluation services and politically corrupted evaluations. Worries about bias control in these approaches increase the importance of subjecting advocacy evaluations to metaevaluations grounded in standards for sound evaluations.

Approach 19: Client-Centered Studies (or Responsive Evaluation). The classic approach in this set is the client-centered study, or what Robert Stake (1983) has termed the responsive evaluation. The label *client-centered* evaluation is used here, because one pervasive theme is that the evaluator must work with and for the support of a diverse client group including, for example, teachers, administrators, developers, taxpayers, legislators, and financial sponsors. They are the clients in the sense that they support, develop, administer, or directly operate the programs under study and seek or need evaluators' counsel and advice in understanding, judging, and improving programs. The approach charges evaluators to interact continuously with, and respond to, the evaluative needs of the various clients, as well as other stakeholders.

This approach contrasts sharply with Scriven's consumer-oriented approach. Stake's evaluators are not the independent, objective assessors advocated by Scriven. The client-centered study embraces local autonomy and helps people who are involved in a program to evaluate it and use the evaluation for program improvement. The evaluator in a sense is a handmaiden who uses evaluation to serve the client's needs. Moreover, the client-centered approach rejects objectivist evaluation, subscribing to the postmodernist view, wherein there are no best answers and clearly preferable values and wherein subjective information is preferred. In this approach, the program evaluation may culminate in conflicting findings and conclusions, leaving interpretation to the eyes of the beholders. Client-centered evaluation is perhaps the leading entry in the "relativistic school of evaluation," which calls for a pluralistic, flexible, interactive, holistic, subjective, constructivist, and service-oriented approach. The approach is relativistic because it seeks no final authoritative conclusion, interpreting findings against stakeholders' different and often conflicting values. The approach seeks to examine a program's full countenance and prizes the collection and reporting of multiple, often conflicting perspectives on the value of a program's format, operations, and achievements. Side effects and incidental gains as well as intended outcomes are to be identified and examined.

The advance organizers in client-centered evaluations are stakeholders' concerns and issues in the program itself, as well as the program's rationale,

Table 7: Comparison of the Three Improvement/Accountability Evaluation Approaches on Most Common ADVANCE ORGANIZERS

Advance Organizers	Evaluation Approaches		
	16. Decision/ Accountability	17. Consumer Orientation	18. Accreditation
Decision makers/ stakeholders	✓		
Decision situations	✓		
Program accountability requirements	✓		✓
Needs, problems, opportunities	✓	✓	
Competing program approaches	✓	✓	
Program operations	✓	✓	✓
Program outcomes	✓	✓	✓
Cost-effectiveness	✓	✓	
Assessed needs	✓	✓	
Societal values	✓	✓	
Intrinsic criteria of merit		✓	✓
Accreditation guidelines & criteria			✓

Table 8: Comparison of the Primary PURPOSES of the Three Improvement/Accountability Evaluation Approaches

Purposes	Evaluation Approaches		
	16. Decision/ Accountability	17. Consumer Orientation	18. Accreditation
Provide a knowledge & value base for decisions	✓	✓	
Judge alternatives	✓	✓	
Approve/recommend professional services			✓

Table 9: Comparison of the Improvement/Accountability Evaluation Approaches on Characteristic EVALUATION QUESTIONS

Characteristic Evaluation Questions	Evaluation Approaches		
	16. Decision/ Accountability	17. Consumer Orientation	18. Accreditation
What consumer needs should be addressed?	✓	✓	
What alternatives are available to address the needs & what are their comparative merits?	✓	✓	
What plan should guide the program?	✓		
What facilities, materials, and equipment are needed?	✓		
Who should conduct the program & what roles should the different participants carry out?	✓		
Is the program working & should it be revised?	✓	✓	✓
How can the program be improved?	✓		✓
Is the program reaching all the rightful beneficiaries?	✓		
What are the outcomes?	✓	✓	✓
Did staff responsibly & effectively discharge their program responsibilities?	✓		
Is the program superior to critical competitors?	✓	✓	
Is the program worth the required investment?	✓	✓	
Is the program meeting minimum accreditation requirements?			✓

Table 10: Comparison of Main METHODS of the Three Improvement/Accountability Evaluation Approaches

Evaluation Methods	Evaluation Approaches		
	16. Decision/ Accountability	*17. Consumer Orientation*	*18. Accreditation*
Surveys	✓		
Needs assessments	✓	✓	
Case studies	✓		
Advocate teams	✓		
Observations	✓		✓
Interviews	✓	✓	✓
Resident evaluators	✓		
Quasi experiments	✓	✓	
Experiments	✓	✓	
Checklists	✓	✓	
Goal-free evaluations		✓	
Modus operandi analysis		✓	
Applying codes of ethical conduct	✓	✓	
Cost analysis		✓	
Self-study			✓
Site visits by expert panels		✓	✓

Table 11: Comparison of the Prevalent STRENGTHS of the Three Improvement/Accountability Evaluation Approaches

	Evaluation Approaches		
Strengths	16. Decision/ Accountability	17. Consumer Orientation	18. Accreditation
Keyed to professional standards	✓		✓
Examines context, inputs, process, & outcomes	✓	✓	
Balances use of quantitative & qualitative methods	✓	✓	✓
Integrates evaluation into management operations	✓		
Targets constituents' needs	✓	✓	
Stresses program improvement	✓		
Provides basis for accountability	✓	✓	✓
Involves & addresses the needs of all stakeholders	✓		✓
Serves decision making at all system levels	✓		
Promotes & assists uses of evaluation findings	✓		✓
Emphasizes democratic principles	✓	✓	
Stresses an independent perspective		✓	✓
Stresses consumer protection		✓	✓
Produces a comprehensive assessment of merit & worth	✓	✓	✓
Emphasizes cost-effectiveness		✓	
Provides formative & summative evaluation	✓	✓	
Grades the quality of programs & institutions		✓	✓
Aided by Scriven's Key Evaluation Checklist & Evaluation Thesaurus		✓	

Table 12: Comparison of the Prevalent WEAKNESSES of the Three Improvement/Accountability Evaluation Approaches

	Evaluation Approaches		
Weaknesses	16. Decision/ Accountability	17. Consumer Orientation	18. Accreditation
Involved collaboration with client/ stakeholders may engender interference & bias	✓		✓
Influence on program operations may compromise the evaluation's independence	✓		
May be too independent to help strengthen operations		✓	
Carries connotation that top decision makers are most important	✓		
May overemphasize formative evaluation & underemploy summative evaluation	✓		
Stress on independence may minimize formative assistance		✓	
Summative evaluation applied too early may stifle staffs' creativity		✓	
Summative evaluation applied too late in a program's process may be void of much needed information		✓	
Heavily dependent on a highly competent, independent evaluator		✓	
May overstress intrinsic criteria			✓
May underemphasize outcome information			✓
Includes many opportunities for evaluatees to coopt & bias the evaluators			✓

background, transactions, outcomes, standards, and judgments. The client-centered program evaluation may serve many purposes. Some of these are helping people in a local setting gain a perspective on the program's full countenance; understanding the ways that various groups see the program's problems, strengths, and weaknesses; and learning the ways affected people value the program, as well as the ways program experts judge it. The evaluator's process goal is to carry on a continuous search for key questions and standards and to provide clients with useful information as it becomes available.

The client-centered/responsive approach has a strong philosophical base: evaluators should promote equity and fairness, help those with little power, thwart the misuse of power, expose the huckster, unnerve the assured, reassure the insecure, and always help people see things from alternative viewpoints. The approach subscribes to moral relativity and posits that, for any given set of findings, there are potentially multiple, conflicting interpretations that are equally plausible.

Community, practitioner, and beneficiary groups in the local environment, together with external program area experts, provide the questions addressed by the client-centered study. In general, the groups usually want to know what the program achieved, how it operated, and how it was judged by involved persons and experts in the program area. The more specific evaluation questions emerge as the study unfolds based on the evaluator's continuing interactions with stakeholders and their collaborative assessment of the developing evaluative information.

This approach reflects a formalization of the longstanding practice of informal, intuitive evaluation. It requires a relaxed and continuous exchange between evaluator and clients. It is more divergent than convergent. Basically, the approach calls for continuing communication between evaluator and audience for the purposes of discovering, investigating, and addressing a program's issues. Designs for client-centered program evaluations are relatively open-ended and emergent, building to narrative description, rather than aggregating measurements across cases. The evaluator attempts to issue timely responses to clients' concerns and questions by collecting and reporting useful information, even if the needed information was not anticipated at the study's beginning. Concomitant with the ongoing conversation with clients, the evaluator attempts to obtain and present a rich set of information on the program. This includes its philosophical foundation and purposes, history, transactions, and outcomes. Special attention is given to side effects, the standards that various persons hold for the program, and their judgments of the program.

Depending on the evaluation's purpose, the evaluator may legitimately employ a range of different methods. Preferred methods are the case study, expressive objectives, purposive sampling, observation, adversary reports, story telling to convey complexity, sociodrama, and narrative reports. Client-centered evaluators are charged to check for the existence of stable and consistent findings by employing redundancy in their data-collecting activities and replicating their case studies. They are not expected to act as a program's sole or final judges, but should collect, process, and report the opinions and judgments of the full range of the program's stakeholders as well as those of pertinent experts. In the end, the evaluator makes a comprehensive statement of what the program is observed to be and references the satisfaction and dissatisfaction that appropriately selected people feel toward the program. Overall, the client-centered/responsive evaluator uses whatever information sources and techniques seem relevant to portraying the program's complexities and multiple realities, and communicates the complexity even if the result instills doubt and makes decisions more difficult.

Stake (1967, 1975, 1999) is the pioneer of the client-centered/responsive type of study, and his approach has been supported and developed by Denny (1978), MacDonald (1975), Parlett and Hamilton (1972), Rippey (1973), and Smith and Pohland (1974). Guba's (1978) early development of constructivist evaluation was heavily influenced by Stake's writings on responsive evaluation. Stake has expressed skepticism about scientific inquiry as a dependable guide to developing generalizations about human services, and pessimism about the potential benefits of formal program evaluations.

The main condition for applying the client-centered approach is a receptive client group and a confident, competent, responsive evaluator. The client must be willing to endorse a quite open, flexible evaluation plan as opposed to a well-developed, detailed, preordinate plan and must be receptive to equitable participation by a representative group of stakeholders. The client must find qualitative methods acceptable and usually be willing to forego anything like a tightly controlled experimental study, although in exceptional cases a controlled field experiment might be employed. Clients and other involved stakeholders need tolerance, even appreciation for ambiguity, and should hold out only modest hopes of obtaining definitive answers to evaluation questions. Clients must also be receptive to ambiguous findings, multiple interpretations, the employment of competing value perspectives, and the heavy involvement of stakeholders in interpreting and using findings. Finally, clients must be sufficiently patient to allow the program evaluation to unfold and find its direction based on ongoing interactions between the evaluator and the stakeholders.

A major strength of the responsive/client-centered approach is that it involves action-research, in which people funding, implementing, and using programs are helped to conduct their own evaluations and use the findings to improve their understanding, decisions, and actions. The evaluations look deeply into the stakeholders' main interests and search broadly for relevant information. They also examine the program's rationale, background, process, and outcomes. They make effective use of qualitative methods and triangulate findings from different sources. The approach stresses the importance of searching widely for unintended as well as intended outcomes. It also gives credence to the meaningful participation in the evaluation by the full range of interested stakeholders.

Judgments and other inputs from all such persons are respected and incorporated in the evaluations. The approach also provides for effective communication of findings.

A major weakness is the approach's vulnerability regarding external credibility, since people in the local setting, in effect, have considerable control over the evaluation of their work. Similarly, evaluators working so closely with stakeholders may lose their independent perspectives. The approach is not very amenable to reporting clear findings in time to meet decision or accountability deadlines. Moreover, rather than bringing closure, the approach's adversarial aspects and divergent qualities may generate confusion and contentious relations among stakeholders. Sometimes, this cascading, evolving approach may bog down in an unproductive quest for multiple inputs and interpretations.

Approach 20: Constructivist Evaluation. The constructivist approach to program evaluation is heavily philosophical, service oriented, and paradigm-driven. Constructivism rejects the existence of any ultimate reality and employs a subjectivist epistemology. It sees knowledge gained as one or more human constructions, uncertifiable, and constantly problematic and changing. It places the evaluators and program stakeholders at the center of the inquiry process, employing all of them as the evaluation's "human instruments." The approach insists that evaluators be totally ethical in respecting and advocating for all the participants, especially the disenfranchised. Evaluators are authorized, even expected, to maneuver the evaluation to emancipate and empower involved or affected disenfranchised people. Evaluators do this by raising stakeholders' consciousness so that they are energized, informed, and assisted to transform their world. The evaluator must respect participants' free will in all aspects of the inquiry and should empower them to help shape and control the evaluation activities in their preferred ways. The inquiry process must be consistent with effective ways of changing and improving society. Thus, stakeholders must play a key role in determining the evaluation questions and variables. Throughout the study, the evaluator regularly and continuously informs and consults stakeholders in all aspects of the study. The approach rescinds any special privilege of scientific evaluators to work in secret and control/manipulate human subjects. In guiding the program evaluation, the evaluator balances verification with a quest for discovery, balances rigor with relevance, and balances the use of quantitative and qualitative methods. The evaluator also provides rich and deep description in preference to precise measurements and statistics. He or she employs a relativist perspective to obtain and analyze findings, stressing locality and specificity over generalizability. The evaluator posits that there can be no ultimately correct conclusions. He or she exalts openness and the continuing search for more informed and illuminating constructions.

This approach is as much recognizable for what it rejects as for what it proposes. In general, it strongly opposes positivism as a basis for evaluation, with its realist ontology, objectivist epistemology, and experimental method.

It rejects any absolutist search for correct answers. It directly opposes the notion of value-free evaluation and attendant efforts to expunge human bias. It rejects positivism's deterministic and reductionist structure and its belief in the possibility of fully explaining studied programs.

Advance organizers of the constructivist approach are basically the philosophical constraints placed on the study, as noted above, including the requirement of collaborative, unfolding inquiry. The main purpose of the approach is to determine and make sense of the variety of constructions that exist or emerge among stakeholders. Inquiry is kept open to ongoing communication and to the gathering, analysis, and synthesis of further constructions. One construction is not considered more "true" than others, but some may be judged as more informed and sophisticated than others. All evaluation conclusions are viewed as indeterminate, with the continuing possibility of finding better answers. All constructions are also context dependent. In this respect, the evaluator defines boundaries on what is being investigated.

The questions addressed in constructivist studies cannot be determined independently of participants' interactions. Evaluator and stakeholders together identify the questions to be addressed. Questions emerge in the process of formulating and discussing the study's rationale, planning the schedule of discussions, and obtaining various initial persons' views of the program to be evaluated. The questions develop further over the course of the approach's hermeneutic and dialectic processes. Questions may or may not cover the full range of issues involved in assessing something's merit and worth. The set of questions to be studied is never considered fixed.

The constructivist methodology is first divergent, then convergent. Through the use of hermeneutics, the evaluator collects and describes alternative individual constructions on an evaluation question or issue, ensuring that each depiction meets with the respondent's approval. Communication channels are kept open throughout the inquiry, and all respondents are encouraged and facilitated to make their inputs and are kept apprised of all aspects of the study. The evaluator then moves to a dialectical process aimed at achieving as much consensus as possible among different constructions. Respondents are provided with opportunities to review the full range of constructions along with other relevant information. The evaluator engages the respondents in a process of studying and contrasting existing constructions, considering relevant contextual and other information, reasoning out the differences among the constructions, and moving as far as they can toward a consensus. The constructivist evaluation is, in a sense, never-ending. There is always more to learn, and finding ultimately correct answers is considered impossible.

Lincoln and Guba (Lincoln and Guba 1985, Guba and Lincoln 1989) are pioneers in applying the constructivist approach to program evaluation. Bhola (1998), a disciple of Guba, has extensive experience in applying the constructivist approach to evaluating programs in Africa. In agreement with

Guba, he stresses that evaluations are always a function, not only of the evaluator's approach and interactions with stakeholders, but also of his or her personal history and outlook. Thomas Schwandt (1984), another disciple of Guba, has written extensively about the philosophical underpinnings of constructivist evaluation. Fetterman's (1994) empowerment evaluation approach is closely aligned with constructivist evaluation, since it seeks to engage and serve all stakeholders, especially those with little influence. However, there is a key difference between the constructivist and empowerment evaluation approaches. While the constructivist evaluator retains control of the evaluation and works with stakeholders to develop a consensus, the empowerment evaluator gives away authority for the evaluation to stakeholders, while serving in a technical assistance role.

The constructivist approach can be applied usefully when evaluator, client, and stakeholders in a program fully agree that the approach is appropriate and that they will cooperate. They should reach agreement based on an understanding of what the approach can and cannot deliver. They need to accept that questions and issues to be studied will unfold throughout the process. They also should be willing to receive ambiguous, possibly contradictory findings, reflecting stakeholders' diverse perspectives. They should know that the shelf life of the findings is likely to be short (not unlike any other evaluation approach, but clearly acknowledged in the constructivist approach). They also need to value qualitative information that largely reflects the variety of stakeholders' perspectives and judgments. However, they should not expect to receive definitive pre-post measures of outcomes or statistical conclusions about causes and effects. While these persons can hope for achieving a consensus in the findings, they should agree that such a consensus might not emerge and that in any case such a consensus would not generalize to other settings or time periods.

This approach has a number of advantages. It is exemplary in fully disclosing the whole evaluation process and its findings. It is consistent with the principle of effective change that people are more likely to value and use an evaluation or any other change process if they are consulted and involved in its development. The approach also seeks to directly involve the full range of stakeholders who might be harmed or helped by the evaluation as important, empowered partners in the evaluation enterprise. It is said to be educative for all the participants, whether or not a consensus is reached. It also lowers expectations for what clients can learn about causes and effects. While it does not promise final answers, it moves from a divergent stage, in which it searches widely for insights and judgments, to a convergent stage in which some unified answers are sought. In addition, it uses participants as instruments in the evaluation, thus taking advantage of their relevant experiences, knowledge, and value perspectives; this greatly reduces the burden of developing, field testing, and validating information collection instruments before using them. The approach makes effective use of qualitative methods and triangulates findings from different sources.

The approach, however, is limited in its applicability and has some disadvantages. Because of the need for full involvement and ongoing interaction through both the divergent and convergent stages, it is often difficult to produce the timely reports that funding agencies and decision makers demand. Further, if the approach is to work well, it requires the attention and responsible participation of a wide range of stakeholders. The approach seems to be unrealistically utopian in this regard: widespread, grass-roots interest and participation are often hard to obtain and especially to sustain throughout a program evaluation. The situation can be exacerbated by a continuing turnover of stakeholders. While the process emphasizes and promises openness and full disclosure, some participants do not want to tell their private thoughts and judgments to the world. Moreover, stakeholders sometimes are poorly informed about the issues being addressed in an evaluation and thus are poor data sources. It can be unrealistic to expect that the evaluator can and will take the needed time to inform, and then meaningfully involve, those who begin as basically ignorant of the program being assessed. Further, constructivist evaluations can be greatly burdened by itinerant evaluation stakeholders who come and go, reopen questions previously addressed, and question consensus previously reached. There is the further issue that some evaluation clients do not take kindly to evaluators who are prone to report competing, perspectivist answers, and not take a stand regarding a program's merit and worth. Many clients are not attuned to the constructivist philosophy, and they may value reports that mainly include hard data on outcomes and assessments of statistical significance. They may expect reports to be based on relatively independent perspectives that are free of program participants' conflicts of interest. Since the constructivist approach is a countermeasure to assigning responsibility for successes and failures in a program to certain individuals or groups, many policy boards, administrators, and financial sponsors might see this rejection of accountability as unworkable and unacceptable. It is easy to say that all persons in a program should share the glory or the disgrace; but try to tell this to an exceptionally hardworking and effective teacher in a school program where virtually no one else tries or succeeds.

Approach 21: Deliberative Democratic Evaluation. Perhaps the newest entry in the program evaluation models enterprise is the deliberative democratic approach advanced by House and Howe (1998, 2000a, 2000b). The approach functions within an explicit democratic framework and charges evaluators to uphold democratic principles in reaching defensible conclusions. It envisions program evaluation as a principled, influential societal institution, contributing to democratization through the issuing of reliable and valid claims.

The advance organizers of deliberative democratic evaluation are seen in its three main dimensions: democratic participation, dialogue to examine and authenticate stakeholders' inputs, and deliberation to arrive at a defensible assessment of a program's merit and worth. All three dimensions are considered essential in all aspects of a sound program evaluation.

In the democratic dimension, the approach proactively identifies and arranges for the equitable participation of all interested stakeholders throughout the course of the evaluation. Equity is stressed, and power imbalances in which the message of powerful parties would dominate the evaluation message are not tolerated. In the dialogic dimension, the evaluator engages stakeholders and other audiences to assist in compiling preliminary findings. Subsequently, the collaborators seriously discuss and debate the draft findings to ensure that no participant's views are misrepresented. In the culminating deliberative stage, the evaluator(s) honestly considers and discusses with others all inputs obtained but then renders what he or she considers a fully defensible assessment of the program's merit and worth. All interested stakeholders are given voice in the evaluation, and the evaluator acknowledges their views in the final report, but may express disagreement with some of them. The deliberative dimension sees the evaluator(s) reaching a reasoned conclusion by reviewing all inputs; debating them with stakeholders and others; reflecting deeply on all the inputs; then reaching a defensible, well-justified conclusion.

The purpose of the approach is to employ democratic participation in the process of arriving at a defensible assessment of a program. The evaluator(s) determines the evaluation questions to be addressed, but does so through dialogue and deliberation with engaged stakeholders. Presumably, the bottom-line questions concern judgments about the program's merit and its worth to stakeholders.

Methods employed may include discussions with stakeholders, surveys, and debates. Inclusion, dialogue, and deliberation are considered relevant at all stages of an evaluation—inception, design, implementation, analysis, synthesis, write-up, presentation, and discussion. House and Howe present the following ten questions for assessing the adequacy of a democratic deliberative evaluation: Whose interests are represented? Are major stakeholders represented? Are any excluded? Are there serious power imbalances? Are there procedures to control imbalances? How do people participate in the evaluation? How authentic is their participation? How involved is their interaction? Is there reflective deliberation? How considered and extended is the deliberation?

Ernest House originated this approach. He and Kenneth Howe say that many evaluators already implement their proposed principles, and point to a monograph by Karlsson (1998) to illustrate their approach. They also refer to a number of authors who have proposed practices that at least in part are compatible with the deliberative democratic approach.

The approach is applicable when a client agrees to fund an evaluation that requires democratic participation of at least a representative group of stakeholders. Thus, the funding agent must be willing to give up sufficient power to allow inputs from a wide range of stakeholders, early disclosure of preliminary findings to all interested parties, and opportunities for the stakeholders to play an influential role in reaching the final conclusions.

Obviously, a representative group of stakeholders must be willing to engage in open and meaningful dialogue and deliberation at all stages of the study.

The approach has many advantages. It is a direct attempt to make evaluations just. It strives for democratic participation of stakeholders at all stages of the evaluation. It seeks to incorporate the views of all interested parties, including insiders and outsiders, disenfranchised persons and groups, as well as those who control the purse strings. Meaningful democratic involvement should direct the evaluation to the issues that people care about and incline them to respect and use the evaluation findings. The approach employs dialogue to examine and authenticate stakeholders' inputs. A key advantage over some other advocacy approaches is that the deliberative democratic evaluator expressly reserves the right to rule out inputs that are considered incorrect or unethical. The evaluator is open to all stakeholders' views, carefully considers them, but then renders as defensible a judgment of the program as possible. He or she does not leave the responsibility for reaching a defensible final assessment to a majority vote of stakeholders—some of whom are sure to have conflicts of interest and be uninformed. In rendering a final judgment, the evaluator ensures closure.

As House and Howe have acknowledged, the deliberative democratic approach is, at this time, unrealistic and often cannot be fully applied. The approach—in offering and expecting full democratic participation in order to make an evaluation work—reminds me of a colleague who used to despair of ever changing or improving higher education. He would say that changing any aspect of our university would require getting every professor to withhold her or his veto. In view of the very ambitious demands of the deliberative democratic approach, House and Howe have proposed it as an ideal to be kept in mind even though evaluators will seldom, if ever, be able to achieve it.

Approach 22. Utilization-Focused Evaluation. The utilization-focused approach is explicitly geared to ensure that program evaluations make an impact (Patton, 1997, 2000). It is a process for making choices about an evaluation study in collaboration with a targeted group of priority users, selected from a broader set of stakeholders, in order to focus effectively on their intended uses of the evaluation. All aspects of a utilization-focused program evaluation are chosen and applied to help the targeted users obtain and apply evaluation findings to their intended uses, and to maximize the likelihood that they will. Such studies are judged more for the difference they make in improving programs and influencing decisions and actions than for their elegance or technical excellence. No matter how good an evaluation report is, if it only sits on the shelf gathering dust, then it will not contribute positively to program improvement and accountability.

Placement of Patton's evaluation approach within the category system used in this monograph was problematic. His approach was placed in the Social Agenda/Advocacy section because it requires democratic participation of a representative group of stakeholders, whom it empowers to determine the evaluation questions and information needs. The approach thus helps the audience gear the evaluation to serve their agenda. Patton gives away authority over the evaluation to increase the likelihood that the findings will be used. However, utilization-focused evaluations do not necessarily advocate any particular social agenda, such as affirmative action to right injustices and better serve the poor. While the approach is in agreement with the improvement/accountability-oriented approaches in guiding decisions, promoting impacts, and invoking the Joint Committee (1994) *Program Evaluation Standards*, it does not quite fit there. It does not, for example, require assessments of merit and worth. In fact, Patton essentially has said that his approach is pragmatic and ubiquitous. In the interest of getting findings used, he will draw upon any legitimate approach to evaluation, leaving out any parts that might impede the audience's intended use.

The advance organizers of utilization-focused program evaluations are, in the abstract, the possible users and uses to be served. Working from this initial conception, the evaluator moves as directly as possible to identify in concrete terms the actual users to be served. Through careful and thorough analysis of stakeholders, the evaluator identifies the multiple and varied perspectives and interests that should be represented in the study. He or she then selects a group that is willing to pay the price of substantial involvement and that represents the program's stakeholders. The evaluator then engages this client group to clarify why they need the evaluation, how they intend to apply its findings, how they think it should be conducted, and what types of reports (e.g., oral and/or printed) should be provided. He or she facilitates users' choices by supplying a menu of possible uses, information, and reports for the evaluation. This is done, not to supply the choices, but to help the client group thoughtfully focus and shape the study. The main possible uses of evaluation findings contemplated in this approach are assessment of merit and worth, improvement, and generation of knowledge. The approach also values the evaluation process itself, seeing it as helpful in enhancing shared understandings among stakeholders, bringing support to a program, promoting participation in it, and developing and strengthening organizational capacity. According to Patton, when the evaluation process is sound and functional, a printed final report may not be needed.

In deliberating with intended users, the evaluator emphasizes that the program evaluation's purpose must be to give them the information they need to fulfill their objectives. Such objectives may include socially valuable aims such as combating problems of illiteracy, crime, hunger, homelessness, unemployment, child abuse, spouse abuse, substance abuse, illness, alienation, discrimination, malnourishment, pollution, and bureaucratic waste. However, it is the targeted users who determine the program to be evaluated, what information is required, how and when it must be reported, and how it will be used.

In this approach, the evaluator is no iconoclast, but rather the intended users' servant. Among other roles, he or she is a facilitator. The evaluation should meet the full range of professional standards for program evaluations, not just utility. The evaluator must therefore be an effective negotiator, standing on principles of sound evaluation, but working hard to gear a defensible program evaluation to the targeted users' evolving needs. The utilization-focused evaluation is considered situational and dynamic. Depending on the circumstances, the evaluator may play any of a variety of roles—trainer, measurement expert, internal colleague, external expert, analyst, spokesperson, or mediator.

The evaluator works with the targeted users to determine the evaluation questions. Such questions are to be determined locally, may address any of a wide range of concerns, and probably will change over time. Example foci are processes, outcomes, impacts, costs, and cost benefits. The chosen questions are kept front and center and provide the basis for information collection and reporting plans and activities, so long as users continue to value and pay attention to the questions. Often, however, the evaluator and client group will adapt, change, or refine the questions as the evaluation unfolds.

All evaluation methods are fair game in a utilization-focused program evaluation. The evaluator will creatively employ whatever methods are relevant (e.g., quantitative and qualitative, formative and summative, naturalistic and experimental). As much as possible, the utilization-focused evaluator puts the client group in the driver's seat in determining evaluation methods to ensure that the evaluator focuses on their most important questions; collects the right information; applies the relevant values; answers the key action-oriented questions; uses techniques they respect; reports the information in a form and at a time to maximize use; convinces stakeholders of the evaluation's integrity and accuracy; and facilitates the users' study, application, and—as appropriate—dissemination of findings. The bases for interpreting evaluation findings are the users' values, and the evaluator will engage in values clarification to ensure that evaluative information and interpretations serve users' purposes. Users are actively involved in interpreting findings. Throughout the evaluation process, the evaluator balances the concern for utility with provisions for validity and cost-effectiveness.

In general, the method of utilization-focused program evaluation is labeled active-reactive-adaptive and situationally responsive, emphasizing that the methodology evolves in response to ongoing deliberations between evaluator and client group, and in consideration of contextual dynamics. Patton (1997) says that "Evaluators are active in presenting to intended users their own best judgments about appropriate evaluation focus and methods; they are reactive in listening attentively and respectfully to others' concerns; and they are adaptive in finding ways to design evaluations that incorporate diverse interests . . . while meeting high standards of professional practice" (p. 383).

Patton (1980, 1982, 1994, 1997) is the leading proponent of utilization-based evaluation. Other advocates of the approach are Alkin (1995),

Cronbach and Associates (1980), Davis and Salasin (1975), and the Joint Committee on Standards for Educational Evaluation (1981, 1994).

As defined by Patton, the approach has virtually universal applicability. It is situational and can be tailored to meet any program evaluation assignment. It carries with it the integrity of sound evaluation principles. Within these general constraints, the evaluator negotiates all aspects of the evaluation to serve specific individuals who need to have a program evaluation performed and who intend to make concrete use of the findings. The evaluator selects from the entire range of evaluation techniques those that best suit the particular evaluation. And the evaluator plays any of a wide range of evaluation and improvement-related roles that fit the local needs. The approach requires a substantial outlay of time and resources by all participants, both for conducting the evaluation and the needed follow-through.

The approach is geared to maximizing evaluation impacts. It fits well with a key principle of change: Individuals are more likely to understand, value, and use the findings of an evaluation if they were meaningfully involved in the enterprise. As Patton (1997) says, "by actively involving primary intended users, the evaluator is training users in use, preparing the groundwork for use, and reinforcing the intended utility of the evaluation" (p. 22). The approach engages stakeholders to determine the evaluation's purposes and procedures and uses their involvement to promote the use of findings. It takes a more realistic approach to stakeholder involvement than some other advocacy approaches. Rather than trying to reach and work with all stakeholders, Patton's approach works concretely with a select, representative group of users. The approach emphasizes values clarification and attends closely to contextual dynamics. It may selectively use any and all relevant evaluation procedures and triangulates findings from different sources. Finally, the approach stresses the need to meet all relevant standards for evaluations.

Patton sees the main limitation of the approach to be turnover of involved users. Replacement users may require that the program evaluation be renegotiated, which may be necessary to sustain or renew the prospects for evaluation impacts. But it can also derail or greatly delay the process. Further, the approach seems to be vulnerable to corruption by user groups, since they are given so much control over what will be looked at, the questions addressed, the methods employed, and the information obtained. Stakeholders with conflicts of interest may inappropriately influence the evaluation. For example, they may inappropriately limit the evaluation to a subset of the important questions. It may also be almost impossible to get a representative users group to agree on a sufficient commitment of time and safeguards to ensure an ethical, valid process of data collection, reporting, and use. Moreover, effective implementation of this approach requires a highly competent, confident evaluator who can approach any situation flexibly without compromising basic professional standards. Strong skills of negotiation are essential, and the evaluator must possess expertise in the full range of quantitative and qualitative evaluation methods, strong communication and political skills, and working knowledge of all applicable standards for evaluations. Unfortunately, not many evaluators are sufficiently trained and experienced to meet these requirements.

The utilization-focused approach to evaluation concludes this monograph's discussion of social agenda/advocacy approaches. The first three of these approaches concentrate on making evaluation an instrument of social justice and modesty and candor in presenting findings that often are ambiguous and contradictory. All four approaches promote utilization of findings through involvement of stakeholders. Tables 13 through 18 summarize the similarities and differences among these approaches in relationship to advance organizers, purposes, characteristic questions, methods, strengths, and weaknesses.

Best Approaches for 21st Century Evaluations

Of the variety of evaluation approaches that emerged during the 20th century, nine can be identified as the strongest and most promising for continued use and development beyond 2000. The other thirteen approaches also have varying degrees of merit, but in this section I chose to focus on what I judged to be the most promising approaches. The ratings of these approaches appear in Table 19. They are listed in order of merit, within the categories of Improvement/Accountability, Social Agenda/Advocacy, and Questions/Methods evaluation approaches. The ratings are based on the Joint Committee *Program Evaluation Standards* and were derived by the author using a special checklist keyed to the *Standards*.[5]

All nine approaches earned overall ratings of Very Good, except Accreditation, which was judged Good Overall.[6] The Utilization-Focused and Client-Centered approaches received Excellent ratings in the standards area of Utility, while the Decision/Accountability approach was judged Excellent in provisions for Accuracy. The rating of Good in the Accuracy area for the Outcome/Value-Added Assessment approach was due, not to this approach's low merit in what it does, but to the narrowness of questions addressed and information used; in its narrow sphere of application, the approach provides technically sound information. The comparatively lower ratings given to the Accreditation approach result from its being labor intensive and expensive; its susceptibility

---

[5]The checklist used to evaluate each approach against the Joint Committee Program Evaluation Standards appears on the following Web location <www.wmich.edu/evalctr/checklists>.

[6]A test to determine differences between overall ratings of models based on one approach that sums across 30 equally weighted standards and the approach used in Table 1 that provides the average of scores for four equally weighted categories of standards (with different numbers of standards in each category) yielded a Pearson correlation of .968.

Table 13: Comparison of the Four Social Agenda/Advocacy Evaluation Approaches on Most Common ADVANCE ORGANIZERS

Advance Organizers	Evaluation Approaches			
	19. Client-Centered Responsive	20. Constructivist	21. Deliberative Democratic	22. Utilization-Focused
Evaluation users				✓
Evaluation uses				✓
Stakeholders' concerns & issues in the program itself	✓	✓	✓	
Rationale for the program	✓			
Background of the program	✓			
Transactions/ operations in the program	✓			
Outcomes	✓			
Standards	✓			
Judgments	✓			
Collaborative, unfolding nature of the inquiry	✓	✓	✓	
Constructivist perspectives		✓		
Rejection of positivism		✓		
Democratic participation	✓	✓	✓	
Dialogue with stakeholders to validate their inputs		✓	✓	✓
Deliberation to determine conclusions		✓	✓	

Table 14: Comparison of the Four Social Agenda/Advocacy Evaluation Approaches on Primary EVALUATION PURPOSES

Evaluation Purposes	Evaluation Approaches			
	19. Client-Centered Responsive	20. Constructivist	21. Deliberative Democratic	22. Utilization-Focused
Inform stakeholders about a program's full countenance	✓			
Conduct a continuous search for key questions & provide stakeholders with useful information as it becomes available	✓	✓		✓
Learn how various groups see a program's problems, strengths, and weaknesses	✓	✓		
Learn how stakeholders judge a program	✓	✓		
Learn how experts judge a program	✓			
Determine & make sense of a variety of constructions about a program that exist among stakeholders		✓		
Employ democratic participation in arriving at a defensible assessment of a program	✓	✓	✓	
Provide users the information they need to fulfill their objectives	✓	✓	✓	✓

Table 15: Comparison of the Four Social Agenda/Advocacy Evaluation Approaches on Characteristic EVALUATION QUESTIONS

Characteristic Evaluation Questions	19. Client-Centered Responsive	20. Constructivist	21. Deliberative Democratic	22. Utilization-Focused
			Evaluation Approaches	
Were questions negotiated with stakeholders?		✓	✓	✓
What was achieved?	✓			✓
What were the impacts?				✓
How did the program operate?	✓			✓
How do various stakeholders judge the program?	✓	✓	✓	
How do experts judge the program?	✓			
What is the program's rationale?	✓	✓		
What were the costs?				✓
What were the cost-benefits?				✓

Table 16: Comparison of the Four Social Agenda/Advocacy Evaluation Approaches on Main EVALUATION METHODS

Characteristic Evaluation Questions	Evaluation Approaches			
	19. Client-Centered Responsive	20. Constructivist	21. Deliberative Democratic	22. Utilization-Focused
Case study	✓			✓
Expressive objectives	✓			
Purposive sampling	✓			✓
Observation	✓			✓
Adversary reports	✓			
Story telling to convey complexity	✓			
Sociodrama to focus on issues	✓			
Redundant data collection procedures	✓			
Collection & analysis of stakeholders' judgments	✓			
Hermeneutics to identify alternative constructions		✓		
Dialectical exchange		✓		
Consensus development		✓		
Discussions with stakeholders			✓	✓
Surveys			✓	✓
Debates			✓	
All relevant quantitative & qualitative, formative & summative, & naturalistic & experimental methods				✓

Table 17: Comparison of the Four Social Agenda/Advocacy Evaluation Approaches on Prevalent STRENGTHS

Characteristic Evaluation Questions	Evaluation Approaches			
	19. Client-Centered Responsive	20. Constructivist	21. Deliberative Democratic	22. Utilization-Focused
Helps stakeholders to conduct their own evaluations	✓			
Engages stakeholders to determine the evaluation's purposes & procedures	✓			✓
Stresses values clarification				✓
Looks deeply into stakeholders' own interests	✓	✓		
Searches broadly for relevant information	✓			✓
Examines rationale, background, process, & outcomes	✓			
Attends closely to contextual dynamics	✓	✓		✓
Identifies both side effects & main effects	✓			✓
Balances descriptive & judgmental information	✓			
Meaningfully engages the full range of stakeholders	✓	✓	✓	
Engages a representative group of stakeholders who are likely to apply the findings				✓
Empowers all stakeholders to influence & use the evaluation for their purposes		✓		
Collects & processes judgments from all interested stakeholders	✓	✓	✓	
Fully discloses the evaluation process & findings		✓		
Educates all participants		✓		

Table 17 (*continued*)

Characteristic Evaluation Questions	Evaluation Approaches			
	19. Client-Centered Responsive	20. Constructivist	21. Deliberative Democratic	22. Utilization-Focused
Both divergent & convergent in searching for conclusions	✓	✓	✓	
Selectively employs all relevant evaluation methods	✓			✓
Effectively uses qualitative methods	✓	✓		✓
Employs participants as evaluation instruments		✓		
Triangulates findings from different sources	✓	✓	✓	✓
Focuses on the questions of interest to the stakeholders	✓	✓	✓	✓
Directly works to make evaluations just	✓	✓	✓	
Grounded in principles of democracy			✓	
Assures democratic participation of stakeholders in all stages of the evaluation		✓	✓	
Uses dialogue to examine & authenticate stakeholders' inputs			✓	
Rules out incorrect or unethical inputs from stakeholders			✓	
Evaluator renders a final judgment, assuring closure			✓	
Geared to maximize evaluation impacts				✓
Promotes use of findings through stakeholder involvement	✓	✓	✓	✓

Table 17 (*continued*)

Characteristic Evaluation Questions	19. Client-Centered Responsive	20. Constructivist	21. Deliberative Democratic	22. Utilization-Focused
Evaluation Approaches				
Stresses effective communication of findings	✓			✓
Stresses need to meet all relevant standards for evaluations				✓

Table 18: Comparison of the Four Social Agenda/Advocacy Evaluation Approaches on Prevalent WEAKNESSES/LIMITATIONS

Weaknesses	19. Client-Centered Responsive	20. Constructivist	21. Deliberative Democratic	22. Utilization-Focused
Evaluation Approaches				
May empower stake-holders to bias the evaluation	✓			✓
Evaluators may lose independence through advocacy	✓	✓		✓
Divergent qualities may generate confusion & controversy	✓			
May bog down in an unproductive quest for multiple inputs & interpretations	✓	✓		
Time consuming to work through divergent & convergent stages		✓	✓	
Low feasibility of involving & sustaining meaningful participation of all stakeholders	✓	✓	✓	✓

Table 18 (*continued*)

Weaknesses	Evaluation Approaches			
	19. Client-Centered Responsive	20. Constructivist	21. Deliberative Democratic	22. Utilization-Focused
May place too much credence in abilities of stakeholders to be credible informants	✓	✓		
Thwarts individual accountability		✓		
May be unacceptable to clients who are looking for firm conclusions	✓	✓		
Turnover of involved users may destroy the evaluation's effectiveness				✓
Empowered stakeholders may inappropriately limit the evaluation to only some of the important questions		✓		✓
Utopian, not yet developed for effective, efficient application			✓	
Open to possible bad influences on the evaluation via stakeholders' conflicts of interest	✓	✓		✓

to conflict of interest; its overreliance on self-reports and brief site visits; and my judgment of its insular resistance to independent metaevaluations. All who use this distinctly American and pervasive accreditation approach are advised to strengthen it in the areas of weakness identified in this monograph. The Consumer-Oriented approach also deserves its special place, with its emphasis on independent assessment of developed products and services. While the approach is not especially applicable to internal evaluations for improvement, it complements such approaches with an outsider, expert view that becomes important when products and services are put up for dissemination.

The Case Study approach scored surprisingly well, considering that it is focused on use of a particular technique. An added bonus is that it can be employed on its own or as a component of any of the other approaches. As mentioned previously, the Deliberative Democratic approach is new and appears to be promising for testing and further development. Finally, the Constructivist approach is a well-founded, mainly qualitative approach to evaluation that systematically engages interested parties to help conduct both the divergent and convergent stages of evaluation. All in all, the nine approaches summarized in Table 19 bode well for the future application and further development of alternative program evaluation approaches.

Summary and Conclusions

The last half of the 20th century saw considerable development of program evaluation approaches. In this monograph, twenty-two identified approaches were grouped as pseudoevaluations, questions/methods-oriented evaluations, decision/accountability-oriented evaluations, and social agenda/advocacy evaluations. Apart from pseudoevaluations, there is among the approaches an increasingly balanced quest for rigor, relevance, and justice. Clearly, the approaches are showing a strong orientation to stakeholder involvement and the use of multiple methods.

When compared with professional standards for program evaluations, the best approaches are decision/accountability, utilization-based, client-centered, consumer-oriented, case study, deliberative democratic, constructivist, accreditation, and outcome/value-added assessment. While House and Howe's (1998) deliberative democratic approach is new and in their view utopian, it has many elements of a sound, effective evaluation approach and merits study, further development, and trial. The worst bets were found to be the politically controlled, public relations, accountability (especially payment by results), clarification hearings, and program theory-based approaches. The rest fell in the middle. A critical analysis of the approaches has important implications for evaluators, those who train evaluators, theoreticians concerned with devising better concepts and methods, and those engaged in professionalizing program evaluation.

A major consideration for the practitioner is that evaluators may encounter considerable difficulties if their perceptions of the study being

Table 19. RATINGS Strongest Program Evaluation Approaches Within Types, Listed in Order of Compliance with The Program Evaluation Standards

Evaluation Approach	Graph of Overall Merit (P F G VG E)	Overall Score & Rating	UTILITY Rating	FEASIBILITY Rating	PROPRIETY Rating	ACCURACY Rating
IMPROVEMENT/ACCOUNTABILITY						
Decision/Accountability		92 (V G)	90 (V G)	92 (V G)	88 (V G)	98 (E)
Consumer Orientation		81 (V G)	81 (V G)	75 (V G)	91 (V G)	81 (V G)
Accreditation		60 (G)	71 (V G)	58 (G)	59 (G)	50 (G)
SOCIAL AGENDA/ADVOCACY						
Utilization-Focused		87 (V G)	96 (E)	92 (V G)	81 (V G)	79 (V G)
Client-Centered/Responsive		87 (V G)	93 (E)	92 (V G)	75 (V G)	88 (V G)
Deliberative Democratic		83 (V G)	96 (E)	92 (V G)	75 (V G)	69 (V G)
Constructivist		80 (V G)	82 (V G)	67 (G)	88 (V G)	83 (V G)
QUESTIONS/METHODS						
Case Study		80 (V G)	68 (V G)	83 (V G)	78 (V G)	92 (V G)
Outcomes Monitoring/Value-Added		72 (V G)	71 (V G)	92 (V G)	69 (V G)	56 (G)

The procedures behind the ratings: The author rated each evaluation approach on each of the 30 Joint Committee program evaluation standards by judging whether the approach endorses each of 10 key features of the standard. He judged the approach's adequacy on each standard as follows: [9–10] [9–10] Excellent, [7–8] [7–8] Very Good, [5–6] [5–6] Good, [3–4] [3–4] Fair, [0–2] [0–2] Poor. The score for the approach on each of the 4 categories of standards (Utility, Feasibility, Propriety, Accuracy) was then determined by summing the following products: 4 x number of Excellent ratings, 3 x number of Very Good ratings, 2 x number of Good ratings, 1 x number of Fair ratings. Judgments of the approach's strength in satisfying each category of standards were then determined according to percentages of the possible quality points for the category of standards as follows: 93%–100% Excellent, 68%–92% Very Good, 50% –67% Good, 25%–49% Fair, 0%–24% Poor. This was done by converting total category score to the percent of the maximum score for the category and multiplying by 100. The 4 equalized scores were then summed, divided by 4, and compared to the total maximum value, 100. The approach's overall merit was then judged as follows: [93–100] [93–100] Excellent, [68–92] [68–92] Very Good, [50–67] [50–67] Good, [25–49] [25–49] Fair, [0–24] [0–24] Poor. Regardless of the approach's total score and overall rating, a notation of unacceptable would have been attached to any approach receiving a poor rating on the vital standards of P1 Service Orientation, A5 Valid Information, A10 Justified Conclusions, A11 Impartial Reporting. The author's ratings were based on his knowledge of the Joint Committee Program Evaluation Standards, his many years of studying the various evaluation models and approaches, and his experience in seeing and assessing how some of these models and approaches worked in practice. He chaired the Joint Committee on Standards for Educational Evaluation during its first 13 years and led the development of the first editions of both the program and personnel evaluation standards. Nevertheless, his ratings should be viewed as only his personal set of judgments of these models and approaches. Also, his conflict of interest is acknowledged, since he was one of the developers of the Decision/Accountability approach. The scale ranges in the above graphs are P = Poor, F = Fair, G = Good, VG = Very Good, E = Excellent.

undertaken differ from those of their clients and audiences. Frequently, clients want a politically advantageous study performed, while the evaluator wants to conduct questions/methods-oriented studies that allow him or her to exploit the methodologies in which he or she was trained. Moreover, audiences usually want values-oriented studies that will help them determine the relative merits and worth of competing programs or advocacy evaluations that will give them voice in the issues that affect them. If evaluators ignore the likely conflicts in purposes, the program evaluation is probably doomed to fail. At an evaluation's outset, evaluators must be keenly sensitive to their own agendas for the study, as well as those that are held by the client and the other right-to-know audiences. Further, the evaluator should advise involved parties of possible conflicts in the evaluation's purposes and should, at the beginning, negotiate a common understanding of the evaluation's purpose and the appropriate approach. Evaluators should also regularly inform participants in their evaluations of the selected approach's logic, rationale, process, and pitfalls. This will enhance stakeholders' cooperation and constructive use of findings.

Evaluation training programs should effectively address the ferment over and development of new program evaluation approaches. Trainers should provide their students with both instruction and field experiences in these approaches. When students fully understand the approaches and gain relevant, practical experience, they will be in a position to discern which approaches work best under which sets of circumstances.

For the theoretician, a main point is that all the approaches have inherent strengths and weaknesses. In general, the weaknesses of the politically oriented studies are that they are vulnerable to conflicts of interest and may mislead an audience into developing an unfounded, perhaps erroneous, judgment of a program's merit and worth. The main problem with the questions/methods-oriented studies is that they often address questions that are too narrow to support a full assessment of merit and worth. However, it is also noteworthy that these types of studies compete favorably with improvement/accountability-oriented evaluation studies and social agenda/advocacy studies in the efficiency of methodology employed. Improvement/accountability-oriented studies, with their concentration on merit and worth, undertake a very ambitious task, for it is virtually impossible to fully and unequivocally assess any program's ultimate worth. Such an achievement would require omniscience; infallibility; an unchanging environment; and an unquestioned, singular value base. Nevertheless, the continuing attempt to address questions of merit and worth is essential for the advancement of societal programs. Finally, the social agenda/advocacy studies are to be applauded for their quest for equity as well as excellence in programs being studied. They model their mission by attempting to make evaluation a participatory, democratic enterprise. Unfortunately, many pitfalls attend such utopian approaches. These approaches are especially susceptible to bias, and they face practical constraints in involving, informing, and empowering targeted stakeholders.

For the evaluation profession itself, the review of program evaluation approaches underscores the importance of standards and metaevaluations. Professional standards are needed to maintain a consistently high level of integrity in uses of the various approaches. All legitimate approaches are enhanced when evaluators key their studies to professional standards for evaluation and obtain independent reviews of their evaluations. Moreover, continuing attention to the requirements of professional standards will provide valuable direction for developing better approaches.

References

Aguaro, R. (1990). *R. Deming: The American who taught the Japanese about quality.* New York: Fireside.

Alkin, M. C. (1969). Evaluation theory development. *Evaluation Comment, 2,* 2–7.

Alkin, M. C. (1995, November). *Lessons learned about evaluation use.* Panel presentation at the International Evaluation Conference, American Evaluation Association, Vancouver, British Columbia.

Baker, E. L, O'Neil, H. R., & Linn, R. L. (1993). Policy and validity prospects for performance-based assessment. *American Psychologist, 48,* 1210–1218.

Bandura, A. (1977). *Social learning theory.* Englewood Cliffs, NJ: Prentice-Hall.

Bayless, D., & Massaro, G. (1992). *Quality improvement in education today and the future: Adapting W. Edwards Deming's quality improvement principles and methods to education.* Kalamazoo, MI: Center for Research on Educational Accountability and Teacher Evaluation.

Becker, M. H. (ed.). (1974). The health belief model and personal health behavior [Entire issue]. *Health Education Monographs, 2,* 324–473.

Bhola, H. S. (1998). Program evaluation for program renewal: A study of the national literacy program in Namibia (NLPN). *Studies in Educational Evaluation, 24*(4), 303–330.

Bickman, L. (1990). Using program theory to describe and measure program quality. In L. Bickman (ed.), *Advances in Program Theory. New Directions in Program Evaluation.*

Bloom, B. S., Englehart, M. D., Furst, E. J., Hill, W. H., & Krathwohl, D. R. (1956). *Taxonomy of educational objectives: Handbook I: Cognitive domain.* New York: David McKay.

Boruch, R. F. (1994). The future of controlled randomized experiments: A briefing. *Evaluation Practice, 15*(3), 265–274.

Campbell, D. T. (1975). Degrees of freedom and the case study. *Comparative Political Studies, 8,* 178–193.

Campbell, D. T. (1988). *Methodology and epistemology for social science: Selected papers* (E. S. Overman, ed.). Chicago: University of Chicago Press.

Campbell, D. T., & Stanley, J. C. (1963). Experimental and quasi-experimental designs for research on teaching. In N. L. Gage (ed.), *Handbook of research on training.* Chicago: Rand McNally.

Chelimsky, E. (1987). What have we learned about the politics of evaluation? *Evaluation Practice, 8*(1), 5–21.

Chen, H. (1990). *Theory driven evaluations.* Newbury Park, CA: Sage.

Clancy, T., with Horner, C. (1999). *Every man a tiger.* New York: G. P. Putnam's Sons.

Cook, D. L. (1966). *Program evaluation and review techniques, applications in education.* Washington, DC: U.S. Office of Education Cooperative Monograph, 17 (OE-12024).

Cook, T. D., & Reichardt, C. S. (eds.). (1979). *Qualitative and quantitative methods in evaluation research.* Beverly Hills, CA: Sage.

Cousins, J. B., & Earl, L. M. (1992). The case for participatory evaluation. *Educational Evaluation and Policy Analysis, 14*(4), 397–418.

Cronbach, L. J. (1963). Course improvement through evaluation. *Teachers College Record, 64*, 672–83.

Cronbach, L. J. (1982). *Designing evaluations of educational and social programs.* San Francisco: Jossey-Bass.

Cronbach, L. J., & Associates. (1980). *Toward reform of program evaluation.* San Francisco: Jossey-Bass.

Cronbach, L. J., & Snow, R. E. (1969). *Individual differences in learning ability as a function of instructional variables.* Stanford, CA: Stanford University Press.

Davis, H. R., & Salasin, S. E. (1975). The utilization of evaluation. In E. L. Struening & M. Guttentag (eds.). *Handbook of evaluation research, Vol. 1.* Beverly Hills, CA: Sage.

Deming, W. E. (1986). *Out of the crisis.* Cambridge, MA: Center for Advanced Engineering Study, Massachusetts Institute of Technology.

Denny, T. (1978, November). *Story telling and educational understanding.* Occasional Paper No. 12. Kalamazoo, MI: Evaluation Center, Western Michigan University.

Ebel, R. L. (1965). *Measuring educational achievement.* Englewood Cliffs, NJ: Prentice-Hall.

Eisner, E. W. (1975, March). *The perceptive eye: Toward a reformation of educational evaluation.* Invited address, Division B, Curriculum and Objectives, American Educational Research Association, Washington, DC.

Eisner, E. W. (1983). Educational connoisseurship and criticism: Their form and functions in educational evaluation. In G. F. Madaus, M. Scriven, & D. L. Stufflebeam (Eds.), *Evaluation models.* Boston: Kluwer-Nijhoff.

Ferguson, R. (1999, June). Ideological marketing. *The Education Industry Report.*

Fetterman, D. M. (1984). *Ethnography in educational evaluation.* Beverly Hills, CA: Sage.

Fetterman, D. (1994, February). Empowerment evaluation. *Evaluation Practice, 15*(1).

Fisher, R .A. (1951). *The design of experiments* (6th ed.) New York: Hafner.

Flanagan, J. C. (1939). General considerations in the selection of test items and a short method of estimating the product-moment coefficient from data at the tails of the distribution. *Journal of Educational Psychology, 30*, 674–80.

Flexner, A. (1910). *Medical education in the United States and Canada.* Bethesda, MD: Science and Health Publications.

Flinders, D. J., & Eisner, E. W. (2000). Educational criticism as a form of qualitative inquiry. In D. L. Stufflebeam, G. F. Madaus, & T. Kellaghan (eds.). *Evaluation models.* Boston: Kluwer.

Glaser, B. G., & Strauss, A. L. (1967). *The discovery of grounded theory.* Chicago: Aldine.

Glass, G. V. (1975). A paradox about excellence of schools and the people in them. *Educational Researcher, 4*, 9–13.

Glass, G. V., & Maguire, T. O. (1968). *Analysis of time-series quasi-experiments.* (U.S. Office of Education Report No. 6–8329.) Boulder, CO: Laboratory of Educational Research, University of Colorado.

Greene, J. C. (1988). Communication of results and utilization in participatory program evaluation. *Evaluation and Program Planning, 11*, 341–351.

Green, L. W., & Kreuter, M. W. (1991). *Health promotion planning: An educational and environmental approach,* (2nd ed.) (pp. 22–30). Mountain View, CA: Mayfield Publishing.

Guba, E. G. (1969). The failure of educational evaluation. *Educational Technology, 9*, 29–38.

Guba, E. G. (1977). *Educational evaluation: The state of the art.* Keynote address at the annual meeting of the Evaluation Network, St. Louis.

Guba, E. G. (1978). Toward a methodology of naturalistic inquiry in evaluation. *CSE Monograph Series in Evaluation.* Los Angeles: Center for the Study of Evaluation.

Guba, E. G. (1990). *The paradigm dialog.* Newbury Park, CA: Sage.

Guba, E. G., & Lincoln, Y. S. (1981). *Effective evaluation.* San Francisco: Jossey-Bass.

Guba, E. G., & Lincoln, Y. S. (1989). *Fourth generation evaluation.* Newbury Park, CA: Sage.

Hambleton, R. K., & Swaminathan, H. (1985). *Item response theory*. Boston: Kluwer-Nijhoff.

Hammond, R. L. (1972). *Evaluation at the local level*. (mimeograph). Tucson, AZ: EPIC Evaluation Center.

Hastings, T. (1976). *A portrayal of the changing evaluation scene*. Keynote speech at the annual meeting of the Evaluation Network, St. Louis.

Herman, J. L., Gearhart, M. G., & Baker, E. L. (1993). Assessing writing portfolios: Issues in the validity and meaning of scores. *Educational Assessment, 1*, 201–224.

House, E. R. (Ed.). (1973). *School evaluation: The politics and process*. Berkeley, CA: McCutchan.

House, E. R. (1980). *Evaluating with validity*. Beverly Hills, CA: Sage.

House, E. R. (1983). Assumptions underlying evaluation models. In G. F. Madaus, M. Scriven, & D. L. Stufflebeam (eds.), *Evaluation models*. Boston: Kluwer-Nijhoff.

House, E. R., & Howe, K. R. (1998). *Deliberative democratic evaluation in practice*. Boulder: University of Colorado.

House, E. R., & Howe, K. R. (2000a, Spring). Deliberative democratic evaluation. *New Directions for Evaluation, 85*, 3–12.

House, E. R., & Howe, K. R. (2000b). Deliberative democratic evaluation in practice. In D. L. Stufflebeam, G. F. Madaus, & T. Kellaghan (eds.). *Evaluation models*. Boston: Kluwer.

Janz, N. K., & Becker, M. H. (1984). The health belief model: A decade later. *Health Education Quarterly, 11*, 1–47.

Joint Committee on Standards for Educational Evaluation. (1981). *Standards for evaluations of educational programs, projects, and materials*. New York: McGraw-Hill.

Joint Committee on Standards for Educational Evaluation. (1988). *The personnel evaluation standards: How to assess systems for evaluating educators*. Newbury Park, CA: Sage.

Joint Committee on Standards for Educational Evaluation. (1994). *The program evaluation standards: How to assess evaluations of educational programs*. Thousand Oaks, CA: Sage.

Kaplan, A. (1964). *The conduct of inquiry*. San Francisco: Chandler.

Karlsson, O. (1998). Socratic dialogue in the Swedish political context. In T. A. Schwandt (Ed.). *Scandinavian perspectives on the evaluator's role in informing social policy. New Directions for Evaluation, 77*, 21–38.

Kaufman, R. A. (1969, May). Toward educational system planning: Alice in educationland. *Audiovisual Instructor, 14*, 47–48.

Kee, J. E. (1995). Benefit-cost analysis in program evaluation. In J. S. Wholey, H. P. Hatry, & K. E. Newcomer, *Handbook of practical program evaluation*, pp. 456–488. San Francisco: Jossey-Bass.

Kentucky Department of Education. (1993). *Kentucky results information system, 1991–92 technical report*. Frankfort, KY: Author.

Kidder, L., & Fine, M. (1987). *Qualitative and quantitative methods: When stories converge. Multiple methods in program evaluation. New Directions for Program Evaluation, 35*.

Kirst, M. W. (1990, July). *Accountability: Implications for state and local policymakers*. In Policy Perspectives Series. Washington, DC: Information Services, Office of Educational Research and Improvement, U.S. Department of Education.

Koretz, D. (1996). Using student assessments for educational accountability. In R. Hanushek (Ed.), *Improving the performance of America's schools*, pp. 171–196. Washington, DC: National Academy Press.

Koretz, D. M., & Barron, S. I. (1998). *The validity of gains in scores on the Kentucky Instructional Results Information System (KIRIS)*. Santa Monica, CA: Rand.

Lessinger, L. M. (1970). *Every kid a winner: Accountability in education*. New York: Simon and Schuster.

Levin, H. M. (1983). *Cost-effectiveness: A primer. New Perspectives in Evaluation, 4*. Newbury Park, CA: Sage.

Levine, M. (1974, September). Scientific method and the adversary model. *American Psychologist, 666–677.*

Lincoln, Y. S., & Guba, E. G. (1985). *Naturalistic inquiry.* Beverly Hills, CA: Sage.

Lindquist, E. F. (ed.). (1951). *Educational measurement.* Washington, DC: American Council on Education.

Lindquist, E. F. (1953). *Design and analysis of experiments in psychology and education.* Boston: Houghton-Mifflin.

Linn, R. L., Baker, E. L., & Dunbar, S. B. (1991). Complex, performance-based assessment: Expectations and validation criteria. *Educational Researcher, 20*(8), 15–21.

Lord, F. M., & Novick, M. R. (1968). *Statistical theories of mental test scores.* Reading, MA: Addison-Wesley.

MacDonald, B. (1975). Evaluation and the control of education. In D. Tawney (ed.), *Evaluation: The state of the art.* London: Schools Council.

Madaus, G. F., Scriven, M., & Stufflebeam, D. L. (1983). *Evaluation models.* Boston: Kluwer-Nijhoff.

Madaus, G. F., & Stufflebeam, D. L. (1988). *Educational evaluation: The classical writings of Ralph W. Tyler.* Boston: Kluwer.

Mehrens, W. A. (1972). Using performance assessment for accountability purposes. *Educational Measurement: Issues and Practice, 11*(1), 3–10.

Messick, S. (1994). The interplay of evidence and consequences in the validation of performance assessments. *Educational Researcher, 23*(3), 13–23.

Metfessel, N. S., & Michael, W. B. (1967). A paradigm involving multiple criterion measures for the evaluation of the effectiveness of school programs. *Educational and Psychological Measurement, 27,* 931–43.

Miron, G. (1998). Choosing the right research methods: Qualitative? Quantitative? Or both? In L. Buchert (ed.), *Education reform in the south in the 1990s.* Paris: UNESCO.

Mullen, P. D., Hersey, J., & Iverson, D. C. (1987). Health behavior models compared. *Social Science and Medicine, 24,* 973–981.

National Science Foundation. (1997). *User-friendly handbook for mixed method evaluations.* NSF 97–153. Arlington, VA: Author.

Nave, B., Miech, E. J., & Mosteller. (2000). A rare design: The role of field trials in evaluating school practices. In D. L. Stufflebeam, G. F. Madaus, & T. Kellaghan (eds.), *Evaluation models.* Boston: Kluwer.

Nevo, D. (1993). The evaluation minded school: An application of perceptions from program evaluation. *Evaluation Practice, 14*(1), 39–47.

Owens, T. (1973). Educational evaluation by adversary proceeding. In E. House (ed.), *School evaluation: The politics and process.* Berkeley, CA: McCutchan.

Parlett, M., & Hamilton, D. (1972). *Evaluation as illumination: A new approach to the study of innovatory programs.* Edinburgh: Centre for Research in the Educational Sciences, University of Edinburgh, Occasional Paper No. 9.

Patton, M. Q. (1980). *Qualitative evaluation methods.* Beverly Hills, CA: Sage.

Patton, M. Q. (1982). *Practical evaluation.* Beverly Hills, CA: Sage.

Patton, M. Q. (1990). *Qualitative evaluation and research methods,* (2nd ed.). Newbury Park, CA: Sage.

Patton, M. Q. (1994). Developmental evaluation. *Evaluation Practice, 15*(3), 311–319.

Patton, M. Q. (1997). *Utilization-focused evaluation: The new century text* (3rd ed.). Newbury Park, CA: Sage.

Patton, M. Q. (2000). Utilization-focused evaluation. In D. L. Stufflebeam, G. F. Madaus, & T. Kellaghan (eds.), *Evaluation models.* Boston: Kluwer.

Peters, T. J., & Waterman, R. H. (1982). *In search of excellence.* New York: Warner Books.

Platt, J. (1992). Case study in American methodological thought. *Current Sociology, 40*(1), 17–48.

Popham, W. J. (1969). Objectives and instruction. In R. Stake (ed.), *Instructional objectives.* AERA Monograph Series on Curriculum Evaluation, (Vol. 3). Chicago: Rand McNally.

Popham, W. J., & Carlson, D. (1983). Deep dark deficits of the adversary evaluation model. In G. F. Madaus, M. Scriven, & D. L. Stufflebeam, (eds.), *Evaluation models.* Boston: Kluwer-Nijhoff.

Prochaska, J. O., & DiClemente, C. C. (1992). Stages of change in the modification of problem behaviors. In M. Hersen, R. M. Eisler, & P. M. Miller (eds.), *Progress in behavior modification, 28.* Sycamore, IL: Sycamore Publishing Company.

Provus, M. N. (1969). *Discrepancy evaluation model.* Pittsburgh: Pittsburgh Public Schools.

Provus, M. N. (1971). *Discrepancy evaluation.* Berkeley, CA: McCutcheon.

Rippey, R. M. (ed.). (1973). *Studies in transactional evaluation.* Berkeley, CA: McCutcheon.

Rogers, P. R. (2000). Program theory: Not whether programs work but how they work. In D. L. Stufflebeam, G. F. Madaus, & T. Kellaghan (eds.), *Evaluation models.* Boston: Kluwer Academic Publishers.

Rossi, P. H., & Freeman, H. E. (1993). *Evaluation: A systematic approach* (5th ed.). Newbury Park, CA: Sage.

Sanders, J. R. (1992). *Evaluating school programs.* Newbury Park, CA: Sage.

Sanders, W. L. (1989). Using customized standardized tests. (Contract No. R-88–062003) Washington, DC: Office of Educational Research and Improvement, U. S. Department of Education. (ERIC Digest No. ED 314429)

Sanders, W. L., & Horn, S. P. (1994). The Tennessee value-added assessment system (TVAAS): Mixed model methodology in educational assessment. *Journal of Personnel Evaluation in Education, 8*(3) 299–311.

Schatzman, L., & Strauss, A. L. (1973). *Field research.* Englewood Cliffs, NJ: Prentice-Hall.

Schwandt, T. A. (1984). *An examination of alternative models for socio-behavioral inquiry.* Unpublished Ph.D. dissertation, Indiana University.

Schwandt, T. A. (1989). Recapturing moral discourse in evaluation. *Educational Researcher, 18*(8), 11–16.

Scriven, M. S. (1967). The methodology of evaluation. In R. E. Stake (ed.) *Curriculum evaluation. AERA Monograph Series on Curriculum Evaluation* (Vol. 1). Chicago: Rand McNally.

Scriven, M. (1974). Evaluation perspectives and procedures. In W. J. Popham (ed.), *Evaluation in education: Current applications.* Berkeley, CA: McCutchan.

Scriven, M. (1991). *Evaluation thesaurus.* Newbury Park, CA: Sage.

Scriven, M. (1993, Summer). Hard-won lessons in program evaluation. *New Directions for Program Evaluation, 58.*

Scriven, M. (1994a). Evaluation as a discipline. *Studies in Educational Evaluation, 20*(1), 147–166.

Scriven, M. (1994b). The final synthesis. *Evaluation Practice, 15*(3), 367–382.

Scriven, M. (1994c). Product evaluation: The state of the art. *Evaluation Practice, 15*(1), 45–62.

Shadish, W. R., Cook, T. D., & Leviton, L. C. (1991). *Foundations of program evaluation.* Newbury Park, CA: Sage.

Smith, L. M., & Pohland, P. A. (1974). Educational technology and the rural highlands. In L. M. Smith (Ed.), *Four examples: Economic, anthropological, narrative, and portrayal* (AERA Monograph on Curriculum Evaluation). Chicago: Rand McNally.

Smith, M. F. (1986). The whole is greater: Combining qualitative and quantitative approaches in evaluation studies. *New Directions for Program Evaluation: Naturalistic Evaluation, 30,* 37–54.

Smith, M. F. (1989). *Evaluability assessment: A practical approach.* Boston: Kluwer Academic Publishers.

Smith, N. L. (1987). Toward the justification of claims in evaluation research. *Evaluation and Program Planning, 10*(4), 309–314.

Stake, R. E. (1967). The countenance of educational evaluation. *Teachers College Record, 68,* 523–540.

Stake, R. E. (1971). *Measuring what learners learn* (mimeograph). Urbana, IL: Center for Instructional Research and Curriculum Evaluation.

Stake, R. E. (1974). *Nine approaches to educational evaluation.* Unpublished chart. Urbana IL: University of Illinois, Center for Instructional Research and Curriculum Evaluation.

Stake, R. E. (1975, November). *Program evaluation: Particularly responsive evaluation.* Kalamazoo, MI: Western Michigan University Evaluation Center, Occasional Paper No. 5.

Stake, R. E. (1983). Program evaluation, particularly responsive evaluation. In G. F. Madaus, M. Scriven, & D. L. Stufflebeam (eds.), *Evaluation models,* pp. 287–310. Boston: Kluwer-Nijhoff.

Stake, R. E. (1986). *Quieting reform.* Urbana, IL: University of Illinois Press.

Stake, R. E. (1988). Seeking sweet water. In R. M. Jaeger (ed.), *Complementary methods for research in education,* pp. 253–300. Washington, DC: American Educational Research Association.

Stake, R. E. (1995). *The art of case study research.* Thousand Oaks, CA: Sage.

Stake, R. E. (1999). Summary of evaluation of reader focused writing for the veterans benefits administration, *American Journal of Evaluation, 20*(2), 323–343.

Stake, R. E., Easely, J., & Anastasiou, K. (1978). *Case studies in science education.* Washington, DC: National Science Foundation, Directorate for Science Education, Office of Program Integration.

Steinmetz, A. (1983). The discrepancy evaluation model. In G. F. Madaus, M. Scriven, & D. L. Stufflebeam (eds.), *Evaluation models,* pp. 79–100. Boston: Kluwer-Nijhoff.

Stenner, A. J., & Webster, W. J. (1971). *Educational program audit handbook.* Arlington, VA: I.D.E.A.

Stillman, P. L., Haley, H. A., Regan, M. B., Philbin, M. M., Smith, S. R., O'Donnell, J., & Pohl, H. (1991). Positive effects of a clinical performance assessment program. *Academic Medicine, 66,* 481–483.

Stufflebeam, D. L. (1966, June). A depth study of the evaluation requirement. *Theory Into Practice, 5,* 121–34.

Stufflebeam, D. L. (1967, June). The use of and abuse of evaluation in Title III. *Theory Into Practice, 6,* 126–33.

Stufflebeam, D. L. (1997). A standards-based perspective on evaluation. In R. L. Stake, *Advances in program evaluation, 3,* pp. 61–88.

Stufflebeam, D. L., Foley, W. J., Gephart, W. J., Guba, E. G., Hammond, R. L., Merriman, H. O., & Provus, M. M. (1971). *Educational evaluation and decision making.* Itasca, IL: Peacock.

Stufflebeam, D. L., Madaus, G. F., & Kellaghan, T. (2000). *Evaluation models,* (Rev. ed.). Boston: Kluwer.

Stufflebeam, D. L., & Shinkfield, A. J. (1985). *Systematic evaluation.* Boston: Kluwer-Nijhoff.

Suchman, E. A. (1967). *Evaluative research.* New York: Russell Sage Foundation.

Swanson, D. B., Norman, R. N., & Linn, R. L. (1995, June/July). Performance-based assessment: Lessons from the health professions. *Educational Researcher, 24*(5), 5–11.

Thorndike, R. L. (1971). *Educational measurement* (2nd ed.). Washington, DC: American Council on Education.

Torrance, H. (1993). Combining measurement-driven instruction with authentic assessment: Some initial observations of national assessment in England and Wales. *Educational Evaluation and Policy Analysis, 15,* 81–90.

Torres, R. T. (1991). Improving the quality of internal evaluation: The evaluator as consultant mediator. *Evaluation and Program Planning, 14*(1), 189–198.

Travers, R. (1977, October). Presentation in a seminar at the Western Michigan University Evaluation Center, Kalamazoo, MI.

Tsang, M. C. (1997, Winter). Cost analysis for improved educational policymaking and evaluation. *Educational Evaluation and Policy Analysis, 19*(4), 318–324.

Tyler, R. W. (1942). General statement on evaluation. *Journal of Educational Research, 35,* 492–501.

Tyler, R. W. (1950). *Basic principles of curriculum and instruction.* Chicago: University of Chicago Press.

Tyler, R. W. (1966). The objectives and plans for a national assessment of educational progress. *Journal of Educational Measurement, 3,* 1–10.

Tyler, R. W., et al. (1932). *Service studies in higher education.* Columbus, OH: The Bureau of Educational Research, The Ohio State University.

Tymms, P. (1995). *Setting up a national "value-added" system for primary education in England: Problems and possibilities.* Paper presented at the National Evaluation Institute, Kalamazoo, MI.

Vallance, E. (1973). *Aesthetic criticism and curriculum description.* Ph.D. dissertation, Stanford University.

Webster, W. J. (1975, March). *The organization and functions of research evaluation in a large urban school district.* Paper presented at the annual meeting of the American Educational Research Association, Washington, DC. (ERIC Clearinghouse on Tests, Measurements, and Evaluation. ED 106 345)

Webster, W. J. (1995). The connection between personnel evaluation and school evaluation. *Studies in Educational Evaluation, 21,* 227–254.

Webster, W. J., Mendro, R. L., & Almaguer, T. O. (1994). Effectiveness indices: a "value-added" approach to measuring school effect. *Studies in Educational Evaluation, 20,* 113–145.

Weiss, C. H. (1972). *Evaluation.* Englewood Cliffs, NJ: Prentice Hall.

Weiss, C. H. (1995). Nothing as practical as good theory: Exploring theory-based evaluation for comprehensive community initiatives for children and families. In J. Connell, A. Kubisch, L. B. Schorr, & C. H. Weiss (eds.), *New approaches to evaluating community initiatives.* New York: Aspen Institute.

Whitmore, E. (ed.) (1998). Understanding and practicing participatory evaluation. *New Directions for Evaluation, 80.*

Wholey, J. S. (1995). Assessing the feasibility and likely usefulness of evaluation. In J. S. Wholey, H. P. Hatry, & K. E. Newcomer. (1995). *Handbook of practical program evaluation,* pp. 15–39. San Francisco: Jossey-Bass.

Wiggins, G. (1989). A true test: Toward more authentic and equitable assessment. *Phi Delta Kappan, 70,* 703–713.

Wiley, D. E., & Bock, R. D. (1967, Winter). Quasi-experimentation in educational settings: Comment. *The School Review,* 353–66.

Wolf, R. L. (1975, November). Trial by jury: A new evaluation method. *Phi Delta Kappan, 3*(57), 185–187.

Worthen, B. R., & Sanders, J. R. (1987). *Educational evaluation: Alternative approaches and practical guidelines.* White Plains, NY: Longman.

Worthen, B. R., Sanders, J. R., & Fitzpatrick, J. L. (1997). *Program evaluation* (2nd Ed.) New York: Longman.

Yin, R. K. (1992). The case study as a tool for doing evaluation. *Current Sociology, 40*(1), 121–137.

DANIEL L. STUFFLEBEAM is the McKee Professor of Education and Director of The Evaluation Center at Western Michigan University (WMU). He developed the CIPP Evaluation Model and led the development of the original editions of the Joint Committee standards for educational program and personnel evaluations. His publications include 13 books and about 100 journal articles and book chapters. He received the ERS/AEA Paul Lazersfeld prize, the WMU Distinguished Faculty Scholar Award, and the CREATE Jason Milman Award. His latest book, with George Madaus and Thomas Kellaghan, is Evaluation Models *(Kluwer, 2000).*

INDEX

Absolutism, rejection of, 71–72

Accountability: constructivist rejection of, 74; six broad types of, 19

Accountability/payment by results approach (#4), 18–20, 89; in questions/methods approaches comparison tables, 43–55

Accreditation/certification approach (#18), 4, 61–62; in improvement/accountability evaluation approaches comparison tables, 64–68

Accuracy ratings of strongest program evaluation approaches (table), 90

Action-research. *See* Client-centered studies (#19)

Active-reactive-adaptive methodology. *See* Utilization-focused approach (#22)

Advance organizers (comparison tables): in improvement/accountability evaluation approaches, 64; in questions/methods approaches, 43; in social agenda/advocacy approaches, 81. *See also* names of specific approaches

Advance organizers, definition of, 10

Advisory panels, stakeholder, 57

Advocacy, social. *See* Social agenda and advocacy approaches

Affirmative action factor, 62

Agencies, education accreditation, 61

Aguaro, R., 30

Alkin, M. C., 58, 78

Almaguer, T. O., 23

Alternative program evaluation approaches: importance of studying, 9–10; pending questions on, 2–5; previous classifications of, 10; professional awareness of, 91; writings on, 9

Ambiguous findings, receptivity to, 70

American Educational Research Association, 2

Annual testing. *See* Outcome evaluation as value-added assessment (#6)

Audiences, evaluation approach. *See* names of specific approaches

Baker, E. L., 25

Bandura, A., 37

Bayless, D., 30

Becker, M. H., 37

Benefit-cost analysis approach (#10), 31–33; in questions/methods approaches comparison tables, 43–55

Best approaches for 21st century evaluations, 7; analysis and judgments of, 1, 11–12; comments on ratings, 4, 12, 80, 89; ratings table, 90

Bhola, H. S., 72–73

Bias: in decision/accountability studies (#16), 58; in public relations-inspired studies (#1), 13–15, 89; and social agenda/advocacy approaches, 62–63

Bickman, L., 38

Bloom, B. S., 17

Bock, R. D., 27

Boruch, R. F., 27

Bridgman, P., 17

Campbell, D. T., 26

Carlson, D., 33

Case study evaluations (#12), 34–36; best approaches rating, 89, 90; in questions/methods approaches comparison tables, 43–55

Case study examples: charter schools evaluation, 22; federally-mandated field experiment (ESAA), 28–29

Categories of evaluation programs, the four: comparison table groups for three of, 43–55, 64–68, 81–88, 90; discussion of category assignments within, 34, 40, 76–77; improvement and accountability evaluation approaches, 42–62, 64–68, 90, 91; the nine best approaches from, 7, 11–12, 80, 89, 90; pseudoevaluations, 13–16, 89; questions and methods evaluation approaches, 16–42, 43–55, 90, 91; social agenda and advocacy approaches, 62–63, 69–80, 81–88, 90, 91; ten descriptors characterizing each of, 11

Category systems for evaluation approaches, previous, 10

Caveats on assessment of approaches, 12

Certification approach. *See* Accreditation/certification approach (#18)

Charter schools, factors in evaluation of, 22

Checklist, program evaluation, 12, 59, 60. *See also* Program Evaluation Standards, Joint Committee

Chen, H., 38

Clancy, T., 13

Clarification hearing approach (#11), 33–34, 89; in questions/methods approaches comparison tables, 43–55

Client-centered studies (#19), 63, 69–71; best approaches rating, 80, 90; in social agenda/advocacy approaches comparison tables, 81–88

Clients and audiences of evaluations, conflicts among, 79, 91

College Entrance Examination Board (CEEB), 61

Company-managed charter schools, an evaluation of, 22

Comparisons between programs: consumer-oriented, 59; objective school testing used for, 20–22

Comparisons tables, evaluation approach. *See* Categories of evaluation programs, the four; names of specific approaches

Conflict of interest: among stakeholders, 79, 91; the author's, 12, 90

Connoisseur-based studies. *See* Criticism and connoisseurship (#13)

Constructivist evaluation (#20), 71–74; best approaches rating, 89, 90; in social agenda/advocacy approaches comparison tables, 81–88

Consumer Reports magazine, 14

Consumer-oriented studies (#17), 58–60; best approaches rating, 89, 90; in improvement/accountability evaluation approaches comparison tables, 64–68

Consumers Union, 14, 60

Contextual influences: and case study evaluations, 34–36; and choosing evaluation approaches, 3; and situational utilization-focused evaluation, 76–79

Controlled experiments. *See* Experimental studies (#8)

Cook, D. L., 30

Cooperative Study of Secondary School Standards, 61

Cost-effectiveness analysis. *See* Benefit-cost analysis approach (#10)

Cousins, J. B., 3

Credibility, questions of external, 71

Criticism and connoisseurship (#13), 36–37; in questions/methods approaches comparison tables, 43–55

Critics, evaluations by friendly, 14–15

Cronbach, L. J., 27, 57, 60

Cronbach, L. J., & Associates, 79

Cut score standards, test, 24

Database systems. *See* Management information systems approach (#9)

Davis, H. R., 79

Decision making support. *See* Management information systems approach (#9)

Decision/accountability studies (#16), 11, 42, 56–58; best approaches rating, 80, 90; in improvement/accountability evaluation approaches comparison tables, 64–68

Delegation of authority issues, 62–63

Deliberative democratic approach (#21), 74–76; best approaches rating, 89, 90; in social agenda/advocacy approaches comparison tables, 81–88

Deming, W. E., 30

Denny, T., 70

Descriptors, evaluation approach, 11

Desert Storm evaluations, 13–14

Dialectical process. *See* Constructivist evaluation (#20)

DiClemente, C. C., 37

Disclosure of findings, factors affecting, 15–16

Dunbar, S. B., 25

Ebel, R. L., 21

Education system assessment. *See* Outcome evaluation as value-added assessment (#6)

Educational testing-based approaches (#5–7), 20–26, 80, 90

Eisner, E. W., 36

Emergency School Assistance Act program (ESAA), evaluation of, 28–29

Empowerment versus constructivist evaluation approaches, 62, 73

Equal access to educational and social opportunities, 62

Evaluation approach classifications: and analysis, 11–12; previous, 10. *See also* Category systems for evaluation approaches

Evaluation approaches: 20th century expansion of, 8–9; caveats on assessment of, 12; further discussion of, 4–5; improvement or discarding of, 4; the most prevalent, 18; the nine best, 1, 7, 11–12, 80, 89, 90; number of, 3–4; pending questions about, 2–5; philosophical distinctions among, 10; versus evaluation models, 9; the worst or least useful, 7, 89

Evaluation, definition of, 11, 62. *See also* Program evaluation

Evaluation methods (comparison tables): in improvement/accountability evaluation approaches, 66; in questions/methods approaches, 48–49; in social agenda/advocacy approaches, 84

Evaluation Models (Madaus, Scriven, and Stufflebeam), 10

Evaluation models versus evaluation approaches, 9

Evaluation profession. *See* Professional practice of program evaluation

Evaluation purposes (comparison tables): in improvement/accountability evaluation approaches, 64; in questions/methods approaches, 44; in social agenda/advocacy approaches, 82

Evaluation purposes, conflicts among, 79, 91

Evaluation questions (comparison tables): in improvement/accountability evaluation approaches, 65; in questions/methods approaches, 45–47; in social agenda/advocacy approaches, 84

Evaluation Thesaurus (Scriven), 60

Evaluators, roles of. *See* Professional practice of program evaluation; names of specific approaches

Experimental studies (#8), 26–29; in questions/methods approaches comparison tables, 43–55

Expert evaluations. *See* Criticism and connoisseurship (#13)

Feasibility ratings of strongest program evaluation approaches (table), 90

Federal government-sponsored evaluations, 8, 28–29

Ferguson, R., 13

Fetterman, D., 73

Field experiment, a failed, 28–29. *See also* Experimental studies (#8)

Fisher, R. A., 27

Flanagan, J. C., 21

Flexner, A., 25

Flinders, D. J., 36

Formative and summative evaluations, 40, 57, 58, 60. *See also* Decision/accountability studies (#16)

Freedom of information issues, 15–16

Funding, school, 28–29; and benefit-cost analysis, 31–33. *See also* Accountability/payment by results approach (#4)

Gain score and hierarchical analysis of data. *See* Outcome evaluation as value-added assessment (#6)

Gearhart, M. G., 25

Generalizability or specificity of results, 71–72

Glaser, B. G., 38

Glass, G. V., 27, 60

Government-sponsored educational evaluations: federal, 8, 28–29, 33; state, 22–26

Graph of overall merit of strongest evaluation approaches, 90

Great Society, the, 8, 28–29

Green, L. W., 37

Greene, J., 2

Grounded theory. *See* Program theory-based evaluation (#14)

Guba, E. G., 10, 35, 41, 70, 72

Guiding Principles for Evaluators (Shadish, Newman, Scheirer, and Wye), 4

Gulf War evaluations, 13–14

Hambleton, R. K., 21

Hamilton, D., 70

Hasci, T., 1

Hastings, T., 10

Health education/behavior change programs evaluation, 37

Henry, G. T., 5

Herman, J. L., 25

Hersey, J., 37

Heubner, T., 1

Holistic evaluations. *See* Case study evaluations (#12)

Horn, S. P., 21, 23, 24

Horner, C., 13

House, E. R., 10, 74–76, 89

Howe, K. R., 74–76, 89

Human subjects. *See* Experimental studies (#8)

Idealistic approaches, overall weaknesses of, 74, 91

Ideological marketing. *See* Public relations-inspired studies (#1)

Improvement and accountability evaluation approaches, 42–62; best approaches merit ratings, 90

Improvement/accountability evaluation approaches comparison tables, 64–68; advance organizers in, 64; evaluation methods in, 66; evaluation purposes in, 64; evaluation questions in, 65; strengths in, 67, 90; weaknesses/limitations in, 68, 91

Indefensible studies. *See* Pseudoevaluations category

Independent assessment. *See* Consumer-oriented studies (#17)

Industry-oriented information systems. *See* Management information systems approach (#9)

Information, program: illicit withholding of, 15; need for and

availability of, 15–16, 60; openness of evaluation process and, 73, 80; redundancy in collection of, 69–70. *See also* Management information systems approach (#9)

Intervention effect studies. *See* Experimental studies (#8)

Intuitive evaluation. *See* Client-centered studies (#19)

Iverson, D. C., 37

Janz, N. K., 37

Joint Committee on Standards for Educational Evaluation, 4, 11–12, 77, 79, 90

Judicial approach to program evaluation. *See* Clarification hearing approach (#11)

Justice, social. *See* Social agenda and advocacy approaches

Kaplan, A., 26

Karlsson, O., 75

Kearny, ??, 19 (//ED: First initial(s) ??)

Kee, J. E., 32

Kemis, S., 33

Kentucky Department of Education, 19, 25

Kentucky Instructional Results Information System (KIRIS), 26

Key Evaluation Checklist (Scriven), 12, 59, 60 (//ED: This is not an italics title. (as per text).)

Kidder, L., 41

Kirst, M. W., 19

Koretz, D., 19, 25

Kreuter, M. W., 37

"Law of the instrument," 26–27

Law as metaphor for program evaluation. *See* Clarification hearing approach (#11)

Legitimacy of politically controlled studies, 15–16

Levin, H. M., 32

Levine, M., 33

Life skills, student. *See* Performance testing approach (#7)

Lincoln, Y. S., 35, 41, 72

Lindquist, E. F., 21, 27

Linn, R. L., 25

Logic, program. *See* Program theory-based evaluation (#14)

Lord, F. M., 21

MacDonald, B., 70

Madaus, G. F., 10, 17

Maguire, T. O., 27

Management information systems approach (#9), 29–31; in questions/methods approaches comparison tables, 43–55

Massaro, G., 30

Measurement research. *See* Objective testing programs (#5)

Mehrens, W. A., 25

Mendro, R. L., 23

Merit ratings of strongest evaluation approaches (table), 90

Merit and worth of evaluated programs. *See* Improvement and accountability evaluation approaches

Messick, S., 25

Metaevaluation: definition of, 59; example of, 33; importance of, 92; justification for, 63; this monograph an example of, 1

Metfessel, N. S., 17

Methods-oriented approaches. *See* Questions and methods evaluation approaches

Michael, W. B., 17

Miech, E. J., 27

Miron, G., 22, 41
Mixed-methods studies (#15), 12, 39–42; in questions/methods approaches comparison tables, 43–55
Models versus approaches, evaluation, 9
Monetary valuation of outcomes. *See* Accountability/payment by results approach (#4); Benefit-cost analysis approach (#10)
Mosteller, ??, 27 (ED: First initial(s) ?)
Mullen, P. D., 37

Nader, R., 60
Narrative descriptions. *See* Client-centered studies (#19); Performance testing approach (#7)
National Education Association, 22
National Science Foundation, 22, 39
Nave, B., 27
Network analysis. *See* Program theory-based evaluation (#14)
Newman, D. L., 4
Norm-referenced testing. *See* Objective testing programs (#5)
Norman, R. N., 25
Novick, M. R., 21

Objective testing programs (#5), 20–22; in questions/methods approaches comparison tables, 43-55
Objectives-based studies approach (#3), 17–18; in questions/methods approaches comparison tables, 43–55
Objectivist orientations: evaluation approaches with, 56, 60; improvement/accountability approaches, 42–62; rejection of, 63, 71–72
O'Neil, H. R., 25
Outcome evaluation as value-added assessment (#6), 22–24; best approaches rating, 80, 89, 90; in questions/methods approaches comparison tables, 43–55
Outcomes-focused studies. *See* Accountability/payment by results approach (#4); Objectives-based studies approach (#3)
Oversight evaluations. *See* Accountability/payment by results approach (#4)
Owens, T., 33

Parlett, M., 70
Participatory evaluation approaches, 3, 69–80

Patton, M. Q., 41, 76–79
Pawson, R., 3
Payment by results studies. *See* Accountability/payment by results approach (#4)
Performance testing approach (#7), 25–26; in questions/methods approaches comparison tables, 43–55
Peters, T. J., 35, 37
Petrosino, A., 1
Pohland, P. A., 35, 70
Politically controlled studies (#2), 13, 15–16, 89; weaknesses of, 91
Politically democratic approach. *See* Deliberative democratic approach (#21)
Popham, W. J., 17, 33
Positive bias of advocacy evaluations, 14
Positivism, rejection of, 71–72
Postmodernism, 62. *See also* Client-centered studies (#19)
Practitioners (evaluation). *See* Professional practice of program evaluation
Privacy issues, benefit-cost analysis, 32
Problem-solving skills, student. *See* Performance testing approach (#7)
Processes of education, and Deming's approach to program evaluation, 30
Prochaska, J. O., 37
Professional certification. *See* Accreditation/certification approach (#18)
Professional practice of program evaluation: chronological list of writings on, 8–9; implications of this review for, 89, 91, 92
Program evaluation: definitions of, 1, 11; the nature of, 10; seminal and alternative approach writings on, 8–9; as a transdiscipline, 60. *See also* Best approaches for 21st century evaluations
Program Evaluation Standards, Joint Committee, 77, 79; checklist of ten checkpoints representing, 12, 59, 60; compliance of nine strongest program evaluation approaches with (table), 90; the four most vital (listed below table), 90; web site, 12n.4, 59
Program improvement, educational. *See* Improvement and accountability evaluation approaches
Program planning, continuous. *See* Decision/accountability studies (#16)

Program theory-based evaluation (#14), 37–39, 89; in questions/methods approaches comparison tables, 43–55

Propaganda. *See* Public relations-inspired studies (#1)

Propriety ratings of strongest program evaluation approaches (table), 90

Provus, M. N., 17

Pseudoevaluations category, 13–16, 89

Public disclosure issues, 15–16, 62

Public mandate studies. *See* Accountability/payment by results approach (#4)

Public relations-inspired studies (#1), 13–15, 89

Publications on program evaluation: chronological listing of, 8–9; evaluation checklists (web page), 12n.4, 59; NSF handbook, 39. *See also* References

Qualitative-quantitative combined studies: methods used in, 35, 40, 41; the seven approaches (#16–22) using, 39, 42, 56–80. *See also* Mixed-methods studies (#15)

Quasi-evaluation studies, 17, 26

Questions and methods evaluation approaches, 16–17; best approaches merit ratings, 90; methods-oriented approaches (#5–15), 20–42; overall strengths and weaknesses of, 91; questions-oriented approaches, 17–20, 89

Questions and methods evaluation approaches (comparison tables), 43–55; advance organizers in, 43; evaluation methods in, 48–49; evaluation purposes in, 44; evaluation questions in, 45–47; strengths in, 50–52, 90; weaknesses/limitations in, 53–55

Questions, typical evaluation (comparison tables): for improvement and accountability approaches, 65; for questions/methods approaches, 45–47; for social agenda/advocacy approaches, 83. *See also* names of specific approaches

Randomized experiment approach, 3

Ratings procedure for table of strongest program evaluation approaches, 17, 80, 90

Realistic evaluation approach, 3

Relativistic school of evaluation, 62, 63

Report cards. *See* Accountability/payment by results approach (#4)

Research-motivated studies. *See* Experimental studies (#8); Program theory-based evaluation (#14)

Responsive evaluation. *See* Client-centered studies (#19)

Results, payment by. *See* Accountability/payment by results approach (#4)

Retrospective versus proactive orientations, 57

Rippey, R. M., 70

Rogers, P., 1

Rogers, P. R., 38

Salasin, S. E., 79

Sanctions, post-evaluation. *See* Accountability/payment by results approach (#4)

Sanders, W. L., 21, 23, 24

Schatzman, L., 41

Scheirer, M. A., 4

School system assessment. *See* Emergency School Assistance Act program (ESAA); Outcome evaluation as value-added assessment

School testing-based approaches (#5–7), 20–26, 80, 90

Schwandt, T. A., 73

Scores, educational quality and school test, 20–22

Scores and overall ratings of strongest program evaluation approaches, 4, 90

Scriven, G. F., 10

Scriven, M., 10

Scriven, M. S., 59–60, 63

Self-studies. *See* Accreditation/certification approach (#18)

Service-oriented approaches. *See* Client-centered studies (#19); Constructivist evaluation (#20)

Shadish, W. R., 4

"Shed pattern" test score data, 24

Situational evaluation. *See* Utilization-focused approach (#22)

Smith, L. M., 35, 70

Smith, M. F., 31

Social agenda and advocacy approaches, 62–63, 69–80; best approaches merit ratings, 90; overall strengths and weaknesses of, 91

Social agenda/advocacy approaches comparison tables, 81–88; advance organizers in, 81; evaluation methods in, 84; evaluation purposes in, 82; evaluation questions in, 75, 83; strengths in, 85–86, 90; weaknesses/limitations in, 87–88

Stake, R. E., 10, 22, 33, 35, 63, 70

Stakeholders: change and active involvement of, 79; clients, 63, 69–71; consumers, 58–60; cooperation of, 91; democratic participation by, 75–76; disadvantaged participants, 62, 71; empowerment of, 62, 73; as human instruments, 71, 73; kinds of questions from, 56–57; targeted users of evaluation findings, 77; turnover of, 74, 79

Standardized educational tests, 20–22; and value-added assessment, 22–24

Standards for educational evaluation, professional: and accreditation agencies, 61; evaluation approach ratings based on, 4, 11–12, 90; importance of, 7, 11, 92. See also Program Evaluation Standards, Joint Committee

Stanley, J. C., 26, 27

State education systems: performance assessment, 25–26; value-added assessment of, 22–24

Steinmetz, A., 17

Stenner, A. J., 19

Stillman, P. L., 25

Strauss, A. L., 38, 41

Strengths of approaches (comparison tables), 90; in improvement and accountability evaluation approaches, 67; in questions/methods approaches, 50–52; in social agenda and advocacy approaches, 85–86

Strongest program evaluation approaches (table), ratings procedure for, 17, 80, 90

Student outcomes testing. See Objective testing programs (#5)

Stufflebeam, D. L., 10, 17, 57, 90

Subjectivist epistemology. See Constructivist evaluation (#20)

Suchman, E. A., 27

Summary and conclusions, 89, 91–92

Summative judgments of programs, 40, 57, 58, 60

Sunshine laws, 16

Swaminathan, H., 21

Swanson, D. B., 25

Systems analysis. See Management information systems approach (#9)

Tennessee Value-Added Assessment System, 23, 24

Testing program names, educational, 21, 61

Testing-based educational evaluation approaches (5–7), 20–26, 80, 90

Theoreticians, awareness of alternate evaluation approaches by: benefits of, 9–10; and inherent strengths and weaknesses, 91

Theory-based evaluation. See Program theory-based evaluation (#14)

Thorndike, R. L., 17, 21

Tilley, N., 3

Timing of program evaluation, 60; continuous and unfolding, 71–72

Torrance, H., 25

Training programs, program evaluator, 91

Tsang, M. C., 32

Tyler, R. W., 17, 41

Tymms, P., 23

Unintended and intended outcomes. See Client-centered studies (#19)

Utility ratings of strongest program evaluation approaches (table), 90

Utilization-focused approach (#22), 76–80; best approaches rating, 90; in social agenda/advocacy approaches comparison tables, 81–88

Utopian approaches, inherent weaknesses of, 74, 91

Validation, theory. See Program theory-based evaluation (#14)

Vallance, E., 36

Value-added assessment. See Outcome evaluation as value-added assessment (#6)

Value-added measurement, 21

Vermont state education system, 25

Veterans Benefits Administration program, metaevaluation of, 33

Waterman, R. H., 35, 37

Weaknesses of evaluation approaches, 7, 91; pseudoevaluation, 13–16, 89

Weaknesses/limitations of approaches (comparison tables): in improvement/accountability evaluation approaches, 68; in questions/methods approaches, 53–55; in social agenda/advocacy approaches, 87–88. *See also* names of specific approaches

Web page resource, evaluation checklists, 12n.4, 59

Webster, W. J., 19, 21, 23, 58

Weiss, C. H., 38

Welfare, consumer. *See* Consumer-oriented studies (#17)

Whitmore, E., 3

Wholey, J. S., 27

Wiggins, G., 25

Wiley, D. E., 27

Wolf, R. L., 33

Worst or least useful program evaluation approaches, 7, 89

Worth of evaluated programs. *See* Decision/accountability studies (#16); Improvement and accountability evaluation approaches

Writing skills, student. *See* Performance testing approach (#7)

Writings on program evaluation, chronological listing of, 8–9

Wye, C., 4

Yin, R. K., 35

Back Issue/Subscription Order Form

Copy or detach and send to:
Jossey-Bass Inc., Publishers, 350 Sansome Street, San Francisco CA 94104-1342
Call or fax toll free!
Phone 888-378-2537 6AM-5PM PST; Fax 800-605-2665

Back issues: Please send me the following issues at $23 each.
(Important: please include series initials and issue number, such as EV77.)

1. EV _____

_____

_____

$ _____ Total for single issues

$ _____ Shipping charges (for single issues *only;* subscriptions are exempt
from shipping charges): Up to $30, add $5^{50} • $30^{01}–$50, add $6^{50}
$50^{01}–$75, add $7^{50} • $75^{01}–$100, add $9 • $100^{01}–$150, add $10
Over $150, call for shipping charge.

Subscriptions   Please ❑ start   ❑ renew my subscription to *New Directions
for Evaluation* for the year ___ at the following rate:

❑ Individual: $66 U.S./Canada/Mexico; $90 International

❑ Institutional: $130 U.S.; $170 Canada; $204 International
NOTE: Subscriptions are quarterly, and are for the calendar year only.
Subscriptions begin with the spring issue of the year indicated above.
For shipping outside the U.S., please add $25.
Prices are subject to change.

$ _____ Total single issues and subscriptions (CA, IN, NJ, NY and DC
residents, add sales tax for single issues. NY and DC residents must
include shipping charges when calculating sales tax. NY and Canadian
residents only, add sales tax for subscriptions.)

❑ Payment enclosed (U.S. check or money order only.)
❑ VISA, MC, AmEx, Discover Card #_____ Exp. date_____

Signature _____ Day phone _____
❑ Bill me (U.S. institutional orders only. Purchase order required.)
Purchase order #_____

Name _____

Address _____

_____

Phone_____ E-mail _____

For more information about Jossey-Bass Publishers, visit our Web site at:
www.josseybass.com   **PRIORITY CODE = ND1**

OTHER TITLES AVAILABLE IN THE NEW DIRECTIONS FOR EVALUATION SERIES
Jennifer C. Greene, Gary T. Henry, Editors-in-Chief

PE88   The Expanding Scope of Evaluation Use, *Valerie J. Caracelli, Hallie Preskill*
PE87   Program Theory in Evaluation: Challenges and Opportunities, *Patricia J. Rogers, Timothy A. Hacsi, Anthony Petrosino, Tracy A. Huebner*
PE86   How and Why Language Matters in Evaluation, *Rodney Hopson*
PE85   Evaluation as a Democratic Process: Promoting Inclusion, Dialogue, and Deliberation, *Katherine E. Ryan, Lizanne DeStefano*
PE84   Information Technologies in Evaluation: Social, Moral, Epistemological, and Practical Implications, *Geri Gay, Tammy L. Bennington*
PE83   Evaluating Health and Human Service Programs in Community Settings, *Joseph Telfair, Laura C. Leviton, Jeanne S. Merchant*
PE82   Current and Emerging Ethical CHallenges in Evaluation, *Jody L. Fitzpatrick, Michael Morris*
PE81   Legislative Program Evaluation: Utilization-Driven Research for Decision Makers, *R. Kirk Jonas*
PE80   Understanding and Practicing Participatory Evaluation, *Elizabeth Whitmore*
PE79   Evaluating Tax Expenditures: Tools and Techniques for Assessing Outcomes, *Lois-ellin Datta, Patrick G. Grasso*
PE78   Realist Evaluation: An Emerging Theory in Support of Practice, *Gary T. Henry, George Julnes, Melvin M. Mark*
PE77   Scandinavian Perspectives on the Evaluator's Role in Informing Social Policy, *Thomas A. Schwandt*
PE76   Progress and Future Directions in Evaluation: Perspectives on Theory, Practice, and Methods, *Debra J. Rog, Deborah Fournier*
PE75   Using Performance Measurement to Improve Public and Nonprofit Programs, *Kathryn E. Newcomer*
PE74   Advances in Mixed-Method Evaluation: The Challenges and Benefits of Integrating Diverse Paradigms, *Jennifer C. Greene, Valerie J. Caracelli*
PE73   Creating Effective Graphs: Solutions for a Variety of Evaluation Data, *Gary T. Henry*
PE71   Evaluation and Auditing: Prospects for Convergence, *Carl Wisler*
PE70   Advances in Survey Research, *Marc T. Braverman, Jana Kay Slater*
PE69   Evaluating Initiatives to Integrate Human Services, *Jules M. Marquart, Ellen L. Konrad*
PE66   Guiding Principles for Evaluators, *William R. Shadish, Dianna L. Newman, Mary Ann Scheirer, Christopher Wye*
PE64   Preventing the Misuse of Evaluation, *Carla J. Stevens, Micah Dial*
PE61   The Qualitative-Quantitative Debate: New Perspectives, *Charles S. Reichardt, Sharon E. Rallis*
PE58   Hard-Won Lessons in Program Evaluation, *Michael Scriven*
PE53   Minority Issues in Program Evaluation, *Anna-Marie Madison*
PE40   Evaluating Program Environments, *Kendon J. Conrad, Cynthia Roberts-Gray*
PE31   Advances in Quasi-Experimental Design and Analysis, *William M. K. Trochim*